"Renowned theologian and New Te[...]
written a book that makes compelli[...]
for all others interested in a truly bil[...]al theology. Picirilli argues that to construct a truly biblical theology, one should start with the Bible itself as 'the best evidence of God's plan,' believing that 'it is better to infer what God has decreed in eternity, from the Bible's account of how God acted in the history . . . of man and the cosmos' rather than starting with the classical 'decrees' and imposing them on biblical revelation. This Scripture-honoring approach produces powerful and important insights into such thorny issues as God's will, human freedom, and divine foreknowledge. *God in Eternity and Time* merits and will reward every dedicated Christian's rapt and focused attention."

—**Richard Land**, executive editor, *Christian Post*, and president emeritus of Southern Evangelical Seminary and the Ethics and Religious Liberty Commission

"Dr. Picirilli demonstrates how human libertarian freedom is consistent with key divine attributes and actions. In so doing, Picirilli masterfully provides understandable and plausible explanations for complex doctrines such as immutability, timelessness, and foreknowledge, as well as God's work in creation, incarnation, and redemption. This book provides answers to thorny theological questions that concern many Christians."

—**Steve Lemke**, provost emeritus and professor of philosophy and ethics, New Orleans Baptist Theological Seminary

"Certainly, Picirilli brings many fresh ideas in support of human freedom, answering conundrums proposed by determinists of every sort. Perhaps his most striking contribution, however, is to throw the more speculative aspects of systematic theology back upon the surer footing of biblical theology. One might even assert that this book is essentially a hermeneutical guide to the issue of divine sovereignty and human freedom. Clearly and concisely written, the book will straighten out many a crooked argument in the complex debate, and will invite readers to connect with Picirilli's previous works on the Calvinist-Arminian issue."

—**James M. Leonard**, vice president, Society of Evangelical Arminians

"While differing from the Molinist model to which I subscribe, Picirilli offers a well-reasoned and innovative model of the relationship between divine eternity and divine temporality. Grounded first and foremost in revealed theology, Picirilli insightfully argues that the events comprising God's relationships with creatures in time are ontologically identical with those same events in eternity. His model effectively avoids the—in my judgment—erroneous extremes of divine determinism and divine openness. This book will be read profitably by biblical theologians who seek an understanding of God that reconciles the scriptural data on divine sovereignty, divine counterfactual knowledge, divine foreknowledge, and genuine human freedom."

—**Kirk R. MacGregor**, associate professor of philosophy and religion and department chair, McPherson College

"Robert Picirilli has written a pleasant text about the most important subject human beings can discuss—God and his relation to time and eternity. Picirilli is both humble and clear, filled with conviction and with reservation, fully confident in Scripture while warning about our penchant for drawing airtight inferences. He cautioned, '[W]hen we try to define too closely the nature of the infinite God and his attributes, considered apart from the biblical account, our logic is not fully dependable.' The reader will find that immediate interaction—sometimes agreement and celebration, sometimes contemplation of possible alternative constructions—characterizes the reading experience. The author's style invites this kind of conversation with the text. It is fun to read and will help one reason with humility, always deferring to Scripture over philosophy and biblically unwarranted assertions, sometimes even those made by the author—as Picirilli fittingly observes, 'This is especially true when our logical inferences appear to be in conflict with what the Bible actually affirms about God.' How the biblical text relates events in time to a biblically warranted understanding of eternal decrees 'according to the counsel of his will' (Eph 1:11 ESV) will probably occur frequently in these interactions with the text. Arguing for a traditional Arminian understanding of eternal, exhaustive foreknowledge as the only alternative that leaves genuine human freedom, libertarian freedom, intact, Picirilli takes issue with confessional

Calvinism (determinism), middle knowledge, and open theism as outside the parameters of the demands of the biblical text as it relates to creation and the intersection of time and eternity. This will provide some healthy theological exercises for the reader. I heartily recommend this book to all who want to engage a mind-clearing, spirit-elevating, theologically challenging, Bible-endearing exercise that will bear eternal fruit and give great clarity to what is at stake on the several sides of this important discussion."

—**Tom J. Nettles**, visiting professor of historical theology, Southwestern Baptist Theological Seminary

"In this book Robert Picirilli does what he does best: he serves the church by writing about theologically controversial issues in a way that is irenic, clear, and enjoyable to read, all at the same time. Picirilli is one of the few authors I know of who are credentialed in, and have taught, Greek exegesis, theology, and philosophy, and this unique combination is in evidence in this volume. This is the best discussion of these matters from an Arminian vantage point, and Calvinists and Arminians alike will benefit from grappling with Picirilli's winsome and cogent analysis."

—**J. Matthew Pinson**, president and professor of theology, Welch College

"In *God in Eternity and Time*, Robert Picirilli deftly wrestles with the paradox of an infinite God acting within a finite world of space and time. With thoughtful, gracious insight he clearly explains why he rejects both open theism and a hard determinism, carefully examining Scripture to understand how an omniscient God can know everything that will happen and yet his creatures are free to act within the arena he created. This work is essential reading for any Christian seriously studying the grand issues of God's sovereignty and human agency."

—**Hershael W. York**, dean, School of Theology and Victor and Louise Lester Professor of Christian Preaching, The Southern Baptist Theological Seminary

GOD

in
Eternity
and
Time

GOD

in
Eternity
and
Time

A New Case for Human Freedom

ROBERT E. PICIRILLI

B&H
ACADEMIC
NASHVILLE, TENNESSEE

Contents

Part Three: Wrapping Up

PREFACE

My purpose in this work is to explore some of the implications of the stunning fact that the immutable God has created the space-time cosmos we inhabit and the equally stunning fact that this personal God interacts with us humans, likewise personal, in this realm.

In a way, there's nothing all that earthshaking about saying this, or even about the implications I will discuss in several chapters. Why do I write about this, then? The answer is a matter of focus. I propose that theologians—many of them, anyway—may need to adjust their focus.

I say this because theologians, in discussing God and his works, sometimes tend to focus primarily on the concept of God as formulated in metaphysical philosophy rather than on God as he reveals himself in the biblical narrative, mutually and personally influencing and being influenced by the race of human beings he made to bear, or be, his image.

I do not mean to suggest by this that theologians consciously or deliberately exalt philosophical constructs over revelation. I am confident that Bible-believing theologians, at least, intend for the Bible to have first place in their thinking. Nor am I denying that there is a place for what is called "natural theology."[1] I am not a Biblicist in the sense that I think there is

---

[1] Natural theology can be defined (nontechnically) as reasoning about God on the basis of logic and experience rather than drawing directly from Scripture.

nothing to consider but the Bible. I am convinced, however, that careful analysis of the biblical text has priority. What we conclude by natural theology must be understood and interpreted by revealed truth, not vice versa.

When theologians focus on God as defined in himself, in eternal immutability, they end up representing God as he is conceived, all too often, in rationalistic philosophy. They concentrate on things the Bible itself never aspires to define, on theological constructs that the inspired writers of Scripture might not even recognize. These constructs include attributes of God such as his impassibility or aseity or simplicity. Often these attributes are defined in terms that grew out of Greek philosophical logic.[2]

Other examples of theological constructs include the classical definitions of the Trinity or of the theanthropic personality of Jesus Christ. As such, I am not inveighing against theological constructs. Many of them, like the two I have just mentioned, express important theological insights, representing the best we can do in defining *mystery*.

Yet another theological construct that some theologians focus on, in order to understand God and his acts, is the concept of divine decrees. These decrees represent the "decisions" of God in eternity, before the creation of this cosmos.[3] There is nothing wrong with attempting to identify the settled intentions of God lying behind the world he created and how he governs it. But doing so easily leads one to define the world by logically inferred decrees rather than to identify the decrees on the basis of God's acts in time and space as described in the Bible.

There is the rub, and there is the difference in perspective I am proposing.

For the infinite, immutable God of eternity to create, and then to act in, the space-time world that is home to us is absolutely incredible, as I will attempt to show. That means we had better take this world seriously

---

[2] As I trust will become clear, I am not suggesting that we can never go beyond what Scripture affirms in our formulations or applications of scriptural truth. But we always need to ascribe primary authority to the biblical text and its clear implications.

[3] This means logically before, not temporally.

as the real world. It serves as the domain in which God interacts with us, and we with him.

The Bible presents God to us in the context of creation and the biblical narrative that describes how he has governed it in the progress of human history. It does not do this in the form of a systematic or philosophical theology. Instead, it reveals God in action and in relationships. To be sure, he has an overarching plan for this world and for us. But wouldn't it be better if we described that plan in the way he has revealed it rather than in accord with a priori theological concepts? In the Bible, God has revealed himself in the very way he considered most effective, so surely the Bible itself is the best evidence of God's plan and therefore the best source of discerning what it is.

Yes, this has important implications for the long-standing theological argument between determinism and freedom.[4] Determinists focus on the decrees God made in eternity and then interpret the events of this world, including specifically the events described in the Bible, in the light of those decrees as they have defined them. I suggest that it is better to infer what God has decreed, in eternity, from the Bible's account of how God has acted in the history—*his* story—of man and the cosmos.

The same applies to God's foreknowledge, a subject that takes up several chapters of this work. All too often, theologians start with the rational concept of foreknowledge and then offer all sorts of objections, based on apparently logical inferences from the concept, to the possibilities the Bible so strongly insists on. Whether God's eternal decrees or foreknowledge— or anything else God is or has forever—we need to refocus and understand

---

[4] This is not a book about soteriology, about Calvinism versus Arminianism. For that, see Robert E. Picirilli, *Grace, Faith, Free Will: Contrasting Views of Salvation: Calvinism and Arminianism* (Nashville: Randall House, 2002). I am aware that many Calvinists object to being identified as determinists, but even compatibilism, often called "soft determinism," is a form of determinism, holding that determinism and freedom are compatible. Paul Helm acknowledges this in his foreword to Michael Patrick Preciado's *A Reformed View of Freedom: The Compatibility of Guidance Control and Reformed Theology* (Eugene, OR: Pickwick, 2019), ix.

the relationship between these eternal aspects of God's nature and the world he created.

It is the latter—the space-time cosmos—that makes up the story of the Bible. This is the stage on which we play our role (my apologies to Shakespeare), and it is likewise the stage on which God plays his role. Neither of us is merely acting a part. What God is doing in and with the created order, including human beings, exactly matches who he is and what he has planned forever. What God has known forever matches but does not govern the record of his and our acts in Scripture and in our experience.

I must give special thanks to two men who have been of great help to me in this project. Steven Lewis (a grandson to make one proud!), a doctoral candidate at Southern Evangelical Seminary, has read an earlier version of this and offered many useful comments. So has Kevin Hester (PhD, Saint Louis University), who oversees the theology department at Welch College. I will acknowledge their contributions several times in notes in this work. One must not assume, however, that either of them would agree with my presentation.

PART ONE

The Acts of Eternal God in Time and Space

ONE

Speaking about God:
Preliminary Considerations

This chapter introduces the "problem" of speaking about God—of doing theology, in other words. There is something of a duality in the way we use language. This results, at least partly, from the fact that we have only one language to speak about two radically different realms.

On the one hand, we speak about the world we ourselves inhabit, the world of space and time, of bodies and actions that can be observed. Apparently we form our language primarily with reference to this world.

On the other hand, we use the same language to speak about a metaphysical realm that is constituted differently, the realm of God's existence in eternity. God's "world" is not a physical one. It is not marked by the passage of time. He simply is—forever and unchanging. In that realm there is no beginning and no end, apparently not even a before and after.[1] No crossing of space, apparently, no movement from one "place" to another.

---

[1] I am not intentionally reflecting (or disputing) the "eternal now" of Aquinas. God certainly knows the events of this world as they really are, and so he knows the

I've made heavy use of *apparently*. Already the problem for speaking about God has reared its head. Our language is not sufficient to describe what it means for God to be, and never to become, in eternity.

This does not stop us—we are all theologians—from speaking many things about him, often without realizing that when we describe who he is in eternity we are for the most part expressing what is beyond our ability to express. (I say "for the most part" because it is true that Scripture now and then speaks of who he is in himself forever.) We love—theologians love—metaphysical speculation.

I am not campaigning against speculative theology; I enjoy it as much as the next person. However, when we ascribe things to God that go beyond what Scripture says about him, we need to be cautious. What the Bible says in its long narrative from Genesis to Revelation, about God and his inter-action with this world of space and time, may well be more reliable than our metaphysical speculation.

To be more specific, we theologians need to exercise some significant caution in affirming how things we attribute to God are so, or are not so. If for no other reason, the great difference between him as infinite and our human finitude—in addition to the limitations of our language as well as the negative impact of the fall and depravity on our cognitive abilities—ought to make us slow to speak and careful when we do.

This caution need not cause us to go off with Barth into thinking of God as so "wholly other" that we can say nothing understandable about his nature. Nor do we need to adopt a Thomist *Deus absconditus* as though God is hidden from our knowledge.[2] (It may be that neither Barth nor Aquinas would recognize my use of his words. Regardless, such a discussion is for another time.)

---

difference between past, present, and future even though temporal distinctions are not aspects of his own essence.

[2] I do not mean to imply that Aquinas held that we can know nothing about God. He distinguished between "quidditative" knowledge of God, as he is in his essence, and "analogical" knowledge of God, which enables us to say meaningful things about him. See *Summa Theologiae* (hereafter *ST*) 1.13.5–6, where Aquinas said that "no name is predicated univocally of God and of creatures," then "Neither,

Discussing some of the traditional attributes of God will serve to illustrate the problem we encounter when we speak about God and the caution we need. The attributes themselves are well established and beyond question, but we can profit from exploring how we can speak about God in those terms.

Does God Have a Body?

I choose to ease into my subject in a way with which I think not many will disagree: the traditional affirmation that God is incorporeal, which means that he does not have a body, at least not a physical body.[3] The Bible is clear that God is a spiritual being, not a physical one. Jesus's conversation with the woman at the well (John 4) includes a clear statement (by one who ought to know in ways far beyond our ability) that "God is spirit." This means, among other things, that God does not have body parts. He has no eyes, no ears, no hands—for just a few of many possible examples.[4]

However—and this is what is important for my purpose—Scripture attributes body parts to him. The Bible speaks freely of his eyes, ears, hands, and more. To be sure, we have been taught to say, correctly enough, that when we and the Bible say such things about God we are speaking anthropomorphically. An anthropomorphism is, simply, to attribute human form to God. (Or to anything else, like an animal or a machine, for that matter. When I say that my computer "thinks," I am speaking anthropomorphically.

---

on the other hand, are names applied to God and creatures in a purely equivocal sense," and then that "names are said of God and creatures in an analogous sense." All quotations from Aquinas are from his *ST*, accessed at https://www.newadvent.org/summa/1.htm.

[3] That there is such a thing as a spiritual body seems confirmed by Paul in 1 Cor 15:44. My purpose here does not include exploring the meaning of that.

[4] Louis Berkhof, *Systematic Theology* (Grand Rapids: Eerdmans, 1941), 65–66, treats this under the heading "the spirituality of God" and observes that when the Bible refers to God's eyes, hands, or so on, it is "speaking anthropomorphically or figuratively of Him who far transcends our human knowledge, and of whom we can only speak in a stammering fashion after the manner of men." This is more or less typical of standard discussion but strikes me as both true and falling short of the full truth.

Computers do not think at all; they only perform what they have been programmed to perform by people, who do think.)

So far, so good. When we read in Ps 11:4, for example, that Yahweh's
"eyes watch, / his gaze [lit. eyelids] examines everyone," we are sophisticated
enough to know that he does not really have eyes. Isaiah 59:1 assures us that
"the LORD's arm is not too weak to save, / and his ear is not too deaf to hear."
We automatically, almost subconsciously, translate this anthropomorphism
into something more conceptual. God has no such body parts.

So, there is at least a sense in which our words, our speech, about God's
eyes or hands is equivocal, which means that our words have a meaning,
when applied to God, which is different from their meaning when applied
to human beings. Or to say this better, perhaps, we do not mean exactly the
same thing when we speak of God's eyes as when we speak of ours.

And here is where the need for caution arises. As soon as we begin to think
about what words mean, we're at an important place. There is also something
univocal in speaking about God's eyes. Anthropomorphisms express meaning;
they communicate truth.[5] In other words, whatever it means for us to have eyes,
there is something of the same meaning involved in saying that God has eyes.

What, then, does having eyes mean? One thing, of course, is the ability
to see. If we can say that God does not have eyes, can we just as confidently
say that he does not see? Probably not, even though it may be just as anthropomorphic to say that he "sees" as to say that he has "eyes."

I digress a moment to say that I have deliberately chosen the terminology I am using: that such an anthropomorphism is both equivocal and
univocal. I prefer this to the usual use of analogy as a way of describing
how we speak about God, since analogy focuses on similarity, and I think it
best to retain the tension between what is different and what is the same in
words attributed to God.[6] Experimentally, I would suggest that such speech

[5] Paul Helm, *Eternal God: A Study of God without Time* (New York:
Oxford University, 1988), 2, insists that some statements about God are not
anthropomorphic.

[6] I am aware that philosophers and theologians often steer a course between
equivocal and univocal by referring to analogy, saying that speech about God

is equivocal in form and univocal in substance.[7] Any reader for whom this terminology complicates the issue may toss it; the main point stands even if we discard *equivocal* and *univocal*. To speak of God as having eyes is not to be taken as literally true but as an anthropomorphism, yet it is true, insofar as meaning is concerned, to speak of him as having eyes.

So then, when we read Ps 11:4, we had better know that, as the psalmist expressed it, the eyes of the Lord see and test everything we think and do. If there's anything different between his "seeing" and ours, perhaps it's that he "sees" far better than we. His eyesight is perfect. The reach of his hand to save is unlimited. His ears pick up our softest whispers, even when they are mere thoughts. And we are in awe of him for that.

Should I say to a grieving widow, for example, that God has no arms to comfort her, I might well be guilty of blasphemy. It is a wicked person, after all, who says, "God will never see what I do; he has no eyes" (cf. Ps 10:11). The response of the author of Ps 94:8–9 to such vacuous thinking is sharply pointed: "Pay attention, you stupid people! / Fools, when will you be wise? / Can the one who shaped the ear not hear, / the one who formed the eye not see?" We are, after all, in his image, not he in ours.[8]

---

expresses a meaning similar to but neither wholly identical with nor entirely different from what the words mean in our human context. For a brief treatment, see Norman L. Geisler, "Analogy," in *Evangelical Dictionary of Theology*, ed. Walter A. Elwell (Grand Rapids: Baker, 1984), 42–43. I am not critical of that approach but prefer to retain the both/and tension and so to avoid mere similarity and strive for substantial identity in meaning. Brian Leftow, "Eternity and Simultaneity," *Faith and Philosophy: Journal of the Society of Christian Philosophers* 8, no. 2 (April 1991): 179n43), suggests that "so-called analogy theories of God-talk reduce to forms of univocity (or equivocity) theory in the end."

[7] By "substance," here, I mean what something is in its essential nature, whereas "form" indicates the way the essential meaning is expressed in a particular example and that could be different in another example. A dear colleague introduced me to this useful distinction between form and substance long ago. See F. Leroy Forlines, *The Quest for Truth: Answering Life's Inescapable Questions* (Nashville: Randall House, 2001), 496–97.

[8] Kevin Hester commented to me, appropriately, that "the *imago Dei* is an important concept to discuss as it relates to the human capacity for relationship,

Indeed, then, our eyes may be poor and limited editions of his. Whatever it means to us to say that we have eyes and see, it means the same—even more fully—to say that God has eyes to see. Sometimes poetry—if that is what this is—speaks more truthfully and forcefully than prose. And I am not merely affirming a sentimental meaning here; I intend metaphysical meaning, meaning in ultimate reality.

So then, yes, to say that God is incorporeal is to say something important about him. However, to say that his eyes see and test everyone is likewise to say something important about him. And to say the same thing about human beings is to say something that corresponds, significantly, with saying it about God.

To state this another way, affirming that God has no body, as truthful as it is, has little meaning, comparatively speaking, for anything but metaphysical reasoning.[9] Such a statement is a largely a priori affirmation. Speaking relationally rather than metaphysically, the Bible refers to God's body parts so often, and with such important lessons involved, that we need to give those representations their full measure of meaning for life—and for theology.[10]

If anyone, in focusing on the doctrine that God is incorporeal, as true as it is, should do so in such a way as to mitigate the important reality of the biblical truth that God's eyes are on us, it would be better to shift one's emphasis away from the truth that he has no eyes. As I think about it, I cannot remember a single instance in Scripture where the author thereof thought it important to remind us that God has no body.

---

language, and ultimately the possibility of revelation." Email message to the author, August 9, 2020.

[9] Kevin Hester is right in reminding me that there is some value in people's knowing that God does not have a body and so is not limited to any one "place," so that he can be "present" with anyone anywhere.

[10] Steven Lewis, commenting on this paragraph, after emphasizing that speaking about God as incorporeal says something important about him, then aptly remarked, "Whether someone holds that God is corporeal would not change the meaning they recognize in these passages of Scripture."

Does God Have Feelings?

We can pursue the same line of thought, in respect to something else we theologians affirm about God, by turning from body parts to feelings. The Westminster Confession (II.I), speaking theologically, observes that God not only has no body, he has no passions. In other words, God is impassible.

There has long been, and still is, much discussion, for and against, about the impassibility of God.[11] Some agree that he is above feelings, at least in some respects. Some disagree.[12] For this reason, observations on this particular attribute can be brief, limited to comments similar to those about incorporeality. Even so, this contributes to the overall proposal I am developing.

For God to be impassible, or "without . . . passions," as the Westminster divines expressed it, means, if taken at face value, that God has no feelings. Many might express it more softly, saying that he is above transitory emotions—or something like that.

Nonetheless, most who have anything at all to say about impassibility will at least say that—like attributing eyes and arms to God—to ascribe anger and joy, distress and pleasure to God is, again, to speak anthropomorphically. But since we are referring to emotions rather than body parts, *anthropathically* is the word to use.

Those who describe our speech this way will affirm that when we say God is or was angry on some occasion the words do not quite mean the same thing as they do when we say that some human being is or was angry. In other words, to speak of God as angry is to speak equivocally.

---

[11] Indeed, a number of standard theologies do not treat impassibility. Francis Pieper, *Christian Dogmatics* (St. Louis: Concordia, 1950), I:440, for example, only mentions in passing, under the heading of immutability, that God is angry or merciful only "according to the difference in the object of His affection," but this does not really address the question of whether God has feelings.

[12] For a helpful discussion of impassibility, including his own "synthetic solution," see Millard J. Erickson, *God the Father Almighty: A Contemporary Exploration of the Divine Attributes* (Grand Rapids: Baker, 1998), 141–64. I thank Kevin Hester for calling my attention to this thorough treatment of the subject.

An example in Hosea will illustrate. Some of what God said to Ephraim (apparently standing for all of Israel) includes this: "My heart churns within Me; / My sympathy is stirred. / I will not execute the fierceness of My anger" (11:8–9 NKJV). Hosea's speech may be anthropopathic, and even if there is something equivocal in his reference to God's "heart," what he says is also univocal. Israel had better believe—yes, all of us had better believe—that God's anger is aroused by sin, that his heart churns (what an apt expression!) on behalf of people, that his sympathy can be stirred. And we sense ourselves drawn to him in adoration.

This is the real God interacting with real people in the real world. Yes, the language is relational, to some degree. Even so, there is something, even if not everything, in God's anger and love here that corresponds to what we feel in human anger and love. The substance, the meaning of God's words in Hosea, comes through loud and clear.

To be sure, God is clearly not subject to the vicissitudes of our emotional vulnerabilities. However, if we focus on his impassibility in such a way that we lose sight of God's feelings, we have lost something very biblical and important.[13] God is personal and has personal relationships.[14]

We need not doubt the fact that God in himself, metaphysically, is above the changing emotional states that our feelings expose us to. Indeed, I am not arguing for or against impassibility as traditionally conceived in

---

[13] Kevin Hester suggests that Anselm's classic *Cur Deus Homo* and Athanasius's *De Incarnation* speak well to this matter. In direct contrast to what I have said, if we were to focus on "feelings" in God in such a way as to lose sight of his essentially impassible nature, we would also lose something very important to sound theology. We need the biblical God who is both compassionate and above our vulnerable emotions. It is worth noting that some theologians include emotions as part of the essence of personality; see Forlines, *Quest for Truth*, 138, who emphasizes this: "God is personal. Man is personal. The basic thrust of the idea of being created in the image of God is that *man is a personal being*. A person is one who thinks, feels, and acts" (italics original). In a different vein, Helm, *Eternal God*, 57, observes that defining personhood is difficult for philosophers.

[14] Kevin Hester cites Augustine's *De Trinitate* in this regard.

theology.[15] Still, I repeat that the Bible, as far as I recall, never undertakes to assure us that God is not a feeling being, that he has no emotions, that he is never really angry or glad. God's wrath or joy may be much more real than ours. The Bible speaks of God relationally, telling us how to perceive him in terms that communicate true, ultimate meaning to us in the world of time and space and bodies and feelings.

The point is that God really relates to us.[16] A passage like Hos 11:8–9, then, is speaking truth—existential truth but not merely so—to us about God. Metaphysical speculation should not be allowed to mitigate this truth and make it less than it is. What we think about God in eternity must not swallow up, as some sort of secondary truth, what we know about him in time and space from the Bible. God as he relates to us is just as important as God in himself in eternity.

Conclusion: So, What Am I Saying?

What, then, am I saying specifically, as it relates to the rest of this book? First, the realm of God's existence in eternity is radically different from the realm of time and space that God created, made us part of, and acts in. The Bible is usually speaking to us in terms of the latter.

Second, there is truth both in what we say about God himself in eternity and in what we say about him in relation to the world of time and space. Our use of language can be both equivocal and univocal when describing God and his eternal attributes and will. As some theologians like to say, we

---

[15] For a helpful defense of the classical idea of impassibility (and immutability) against the criticism that it makes God static and unsympathetic, see L. Roger Owens, "Free, Present, and Faithful: A Theological Reading of the Character of God in Exodus," *New Blackfriars* 85 (2004): 614–27. He cites Herbert McCabe, *God Matters* (Springfield, IL: Templegate, 1987), to show that critics like process theologians do not understand what classical theologians really mean and that while it is correct to say that God has no passions, it is equally correct to say that God does not *not* have passions.

[16] By this statement I do not mean to refer to Thomas Aquinas's concept of "real relation." That will be mentioned again in a subsequent chapter.

cannot know God exhaustively, but we can know him accurately. The best way to do that is to know him as he is depicted in relationship to, and in the context of, the natural order over which he exercises dominion.

Third, our metaphysical descriptions of God and his acts, in regard to the eternal realm (that he has no body or emotions, for example) may not always seem to cohere logically with descriptions of him in regard to the latter realm (that his eyes observe everything we do or that he is angered by sin). Any apparent incoherence, however, is just that—apparent—and results from the capacity of language to be ambiguous—as well as from our own finite limitations, and fallen nature, in understanding the infinite.

In the end, when the two aspects of our understanding do not seem to cohere, the aspect we must by no means give up is that of the biblical narrative, which speaks—often relationally—about God's actions in time and space as actions in the real world. The chapters to come should clarify this.

TWO

The Immutability of God

The previous chapter briefly touched on two of the traditional divine attributes we affirm in speaking about God: that God is incorporeal and impassible. The discussion showed that (1) they do not mean everything they might logically be taken to mean in some absolute sense; and (2) in the real, space–time world of the biblical record and of our experience, we can say things about God that both fit with such attributes and appear to contradict them, especially if those attributes (or the things we say) are taken to be absolute.

With something of the same idea in mind, discussing yet another attribute of God will demonstrate the ambivalence of speaking about God even more dramatically: the immutability of God and the apparent incoherence between that attribute and his creation of the world. This is a matter of great significance, and attention to it has not measured up to its importance. In introducing the high tension between immutability and creation, I am heading directly for the main thesis of this book.

To begin, the implications of the previous chapter seem even more significant and complex when we deal with God's immutability. This attribute means that "God does not change," and these are the very words of the Westminster Confession that immediately follow the words quoted from it in chapter 1. Evangelical theologians, perhaps without exception, are satisfied that God is immutable. And we are confident we are on sound, biblical footing: "I, the LORD, have not changed" (Mal 3:6).

It is important to affirm immutability; there are good reasons for doing so. That he does not change enables us to have certainty about things like truth and morality. Like God the Son, God is radically "the same yesterday, today, and forever" (Heb 13:8). His essence never changes, nor does the truth of his promises and judgments—and saying these things only begins what could be a lengthy litany of implications.

Questions about Immutability

As with incorporeality and impassibility, so with immutability: the Bible says things that do not seem, at first glance, to be coherent with this attribute. Perhaps the most well-known example of this is the fact that the Bible (at least in the King James Version) often says that God "repents."[1] Genesis 6:6–7, for example, reports that God, seeing the pervasive wickedness of the human race, was grieved in his heart and "repented" that he had made man on the earth. Jonah 3:10 reports that God, after observing the repentance of those in Nineveh, "*repented* of the evil that he had said that he would do unto them" (KJ21, emphasis added).

Regardless of what word we use to translate the Hebrew original, the question is what the Bible means in saying that God repents. Does this contradict immutability? This question has long been a matter of discussion among interpreters of the Bible, including theologians, and I have no new answers to propose. Even so, some observations are in order.

---

[1] Some versions use "relents" or "regrets," words that do not really address the issue. Perhaps such words are used to avoid the idea that God repents of having done something wrong or deficient, which would not be appropriate for God.

The question boils down to asking whether God "changed his mind" about having created the human race or about how he would deal with Nineveh in Jonah's day. When we say that a human being repents, that is what we mean: that the person has changed his or her mind. The Greek word translated "repent" (*metanoeō*), used both in the New Testament and in the Greek Old Testament (Septuagint), literally means to change one's way of thinking.[2] On the surface, at least, this certainly sounds like a change in God.

Some are quick to temper the Bible's words by suggesting that the language is phenomenal; that is, "The phenomena are such as, in the case of a man, would indicate a change of mind."[3] Probably this is similar to saying that the language is equivocal. At any rate, this statement seems sensible enough, although it begs the question of whether biblical affirmations that God repented mean that he changed his mind. Anthropopathism is at work again. Saying that God repented is attributing to him what a human being would be doing in acting the way God acted in these situations. Indeed, the language of Gen 6:6–7 is both anthropopathic and anthropomorphic in saying that God was grieved in his heart and repented that he had made man. God has no heart. (What a terrible thing to say!)

Then perhaps the things already said need saying again. When we claim that God changes his mind, or repents, we are speaking equivocally; we are saying something that does not mean exactly the same thing, literally, when applied to God. But we are also speaking univocally; what we say is true, at one level of meaning, of God. There is something in what God is doing that corresponds to what we do when we change our minds. Speaking relationally, at least, God really repents, depending on human response. That is the truth, and it is a truth every bit as significant for theology as the truth that God is immutable and never changes his mind.

---

[2] This is the word used in the Greek version of Jonah but not in Gen 6:6, where the wording is somewhat different but the meaning similar.

[3] *The Scofield Bible*, in a note on Zech 8:14. Forlines, *Quest for Truth*, 70 (see chap. 1, n. 7), says this means that God changed his attitude toward the Ninevites in response to their change of attitude toward him, adding: "He is unchangeably committed to change His attitude toward those who change their attitude toward Him."

We are hard-pressed to find wording that states such things satisfactorily. It would not be appropriate, apparently, to suggest that there is sorrow or regret in God when he "repents" (2 Cor 7:10) or that he has done anything wrong to be repented. Instead, such situations are understood by us to represent a change, from what God was about to do, to a different course of action, as he responds to human choices. This represents no real change in the nature of God but frames as conditional God's sincere pronouncements in these cases, even when their conditional nature is not stated.

The Infinite Perfections of the Immutable God

Indeed, this discussion brings us to a very real question: Can an infinite and immutable God act at all? If really changing his mind about what to do (as in the case of Nineveh) is a violation of immutability, is not any "doing"—at least in this space–time world—also a violation of that attribute? In other words, can God "do" anything in this world, anything bounded by space and time, anything he does not "do" eternally?

To appreciate this question fully, one should look carefully at the infinite perfection of God as contemplated in immutability. God cannot change because he is already, eternally, everything he can be.[4] He can become nothing he is not already. He is perfect and complete in every respect, and we need to recognize the implications of this state of being. For this fact to sink in—and overwhelm us, as it should—we ought to consider closely some of the implications of his perfections, of the immutability of the infinite God.

God's works within himself will make a good starting point.[5] One example to consider is the relationships that exist between the Father, the

---

[4] What does the word *change* mean? Perhaps the definition of Stephen T. Davis, *Logic and the Nature of God* (London: Macmillan, 1983), 42–44, is as good as any: "to change includes (1) a change in relations with another thing; (2) a change in position or location; (3) a change in age (temporal change); or (4) having some other 'property' at one time and not another (alteration), this last being the sense of change involved in the immutability of God."

[5] Some theologians call these *opera ad intra*, in contrast to *opera ad extra*. See, for example, Louis Berkhof, *Systematic Theology* (Grand Rapids: Eerdmans, 1949), 89.

Son, and the Holy Spirit, whatever those relationships are. Traditionally, some speak of the Son as "eternally begotten" by the Father, and of the Spirit as "eternally proceeding" from the Father and the Son.[6] Such a theological construct—and it is a logical construct—can be, and is, debated, and it is not necessary to insist on this terminology. What is necessary, however, is this: if the Second Person of the Trinity is "begotten" by the First Person, that begetting must be an eternal begetting. It can never have begun or ended, else that would amount to a change in the nature of God.

That matter is complicated, for sure, and some simplification may help us understand. We can surely agree to speak of the love that exists between the Father and the Son and the Spirit, or of their sharing the same essence and purpose. Whatever those internal relationships are, they must, by definition, be eternal. God is eternally triune, perfect in that tri-unity, never changing. He "does not change like shifting shadows" (Jas 1:17), there is "no variation or shadow due to change" (ESV).

This much is clear and unconfusing. It prepares us to think about other implications of his unchanging perfections. Consider, then, that the God who does not change is eternally, perfectly satisfied and fulfilled, desiring nothing other than what he desires—and possesses—forever. He is absolutely complete in himself, and the trinitarian interaction just mentioned is but one aspect of that completeness. Nothing will complete him; nothing can be added. He needs nothing. There is no potential in him, no becoming. No improvement to his circumstances—if it is appropriate to speak of God's "circumstances" in eternal self-existence—can even be conceived, much less the opposite of improvement. If these things were not so, he would be subject to change. Instead, he is eternally everything he can be.

I do not believe I have exaggerated this. I suspect, rather, that any expression about God's immutable perfections is doomed to say less than the truth about him, not more. At any rate, a full comprehension of who God is in eternity is clearly beyond our ability and raises any number of questions.

---

[6] For a somewhat tedious discussion of these activities, see W. G. T. Shedd, *Dogmatic Theology*, 2 vols. (Grand Rapids: Zondervan, n.d.), 1:286–96.

What does it mean for God to be without change eternally? The Bible does not undertake to answer such questions, other than to give us a hint here and there. We and our experiences are too limited to allow us to answer the question. Logical speculation is always possible, of course, although such speculation must be recognized for what it is. The very idea of an eternally unchanging God is mind-boggling. Even so, this truth has some important logical implications.

One thing that seems clear enough is that God alone is this eternally unchanging being. By definition of the word *God*, as a priori as it is to define him, he must be immutable and eternal. Consider logically, then, that this God has no beginning or end; he simply is. He is forever, and he cannot change. Perhaps such an ineffable Being ought not to be pictured, but for the sake of a mental concept we might try to picture or conceive of God as a being who is there forever, never changing, so complete in every way that nothing can or will complement, improve, or lessen him, so satisfied that nothing can increase or decrease his pleasure.

Again, I do not believe I have exaggerated. To be sure, constructing this description goes beyond biblical language. This is a theo-logical construct, but then again so are our affirmations that God is incorporeal or impassible or immutable or a Trinity. The logical implications of such constructs are always there to tempt us. To express God's immutability in this way raises questions, but those questions are not meant to destroy the constructs.

Once we affirm that God is infinitely perfect and without change forever, the most basic question that occurs is simply this: How, then, can anything else exist at all? (I am asking logically and rhetorically, not biblically.) If only the God who needs nothing exists forever, anything else must be brought into existence by him—and that is, of course, the case. Nothing other than God exists on its own or apart from his creating and upholding power. But there appears to be no logical reason for such a God in eternity to create anything or anyone else. We know from the Bible that he has created existing entities that do not share his deity—beings that are "other than" God—but there's something about this fact that is not quite coherent, logically, with an immutable, eternal, infinitely perfect, self-satisfied God.

Once we begin thinking along these lines, a number of questions arise. Some we can ask without intending to imply any certain answer. For example, can the God who does not change carry on the kind of mental activity we humans carry on? We "think things through," starting with one idea and developing it—much as I am doing in developing this book. All such mental movement and invention apparently represents change.

If mental invention is change, can God come up with an idea? What seems logical is that he cannot think of anything or reach any conclusion he has not thought of or concluded forever. He can't "learn" anything because he already knows everything; surely his omniscience requires us to say this. To learn anything, to gain knowledge, represents change. (God's knowledge in respect to the space–time world and in relation to eternity will make up an important topic of discussion later in this book.)

One question leads to another: Can God make what we call "decisions"? To make a decision, it seems, is to arrive at a conclusion, and that calls for change, for something new in our mental processes and behavior. Perhaps there is such a thing as an "eternal" decision? Like eternally begetting the Son? In asking this I am not intentionally being humorous or ridiculing the idea. I am intentionally raising questions that seem impossible to answer. Perhaps to attribute decisions to God is to speak anthropopathically again, to speak both equivocally and univocally.

At any rate, if God does not change, it would appear that he experiences no "processes," mental or otherwise, unless he experiences them forever. Indeed, can God experience anything he has not experienced eternally? To do so, it seems, would be to change.

In that case, can he act at all, except perhaps as he acts eternally? Can he do anything he does not do forever, whether thinking, deciding, knowing, or willing? And if he can, is that change?

Indeed, is God helpless? Well, the God who needs nothing and is already perfect cannot become anything he is not already. He is already everything

he can be, so there is no help for him outside himself. And even within himself if he "helps" himself be perfect, he must do so forever.[7]

So, what do all these conundrums—if that's what they are—leave us
with? The skeptical philosopher David Hume complained, "A mind, whose
acts and sentiments and ideas are not distinct and successive," who is "wholly
simple, and wholly immutable, is a mind, which has no thought, no reason,
no will, no sentiment, no love, no hatred; or in a word, is no mind at all."[8]
Is that what we are left with? Is God a fixed, "frozen" being who can neither
be influenced nor respond? He is not, of course, but how do we get from
immutability to this answer?

Such discussion may well intrude into the very nature of God, and
we are not equipped—logically or otherwise—for that. The veil before the
Holy of Holies that is the inner being of God himself has not yet been torn
apart to give us access. All our logic, all our experience, must bow before his
holy transcendence. We are grateful that we have the Bible as God's authori-
tative word, as well as the God-given powers of observation and reason,
along with the Spirit's enlightenment, to help us understand God and his
ways. We can depend on God's self-revelation, the sacred Scriptures.

The Bible answers some—not all—of our questions in ways that do not
match the logical implications of everything we say in our theology. I am
convinced that everything I have said about immutability in this chapter,
including the implications of the questions I have raised, is logically inherent in the concept of immutability. To whatever degree I am right in this,

---

[7] I trust that you understand the rhetorical nature of most of these questions.
God is not "helpless" in the way we usually use that word. I am attempting to
explore the full, logical implications of immutability, suggesting the kind of questions that I think cannot be avoided but that usually are. No doubt, as Steven Lewis
reminds me, God is always perfectly free to act in any way he chooses, but that does
not say how this fits in with a robust concept of immutability. (There! I've used
"robust," fulfilling what is apparently a universal demand on biblical-theological
writers these days!)

[8] David Hume, "Dialogues Concerning Natural Religion," in *Hume on
Religion*, ed. R. Wollheim (London: n.p., 1963), 133, cited in Helm, *Eternal God*,
57 (see chap. 1, n. 5).

the required response is to recognize that attributes like immutability are not intended to be taken to mean every single thing they are capable of meaning, or that every possible conclusion that can be logically drawn from them is dependable. What the Bible says about God and his acts is far more important than our theological constructs, including divine immutability. And when we draw implications from the doctrine of immutability, we will inevitably speak both equivocally and univocally.

I am not decrying speculative theology. I myself enjoy doing some of that. Indeed, I will offer at least one chapter in this volume that offers a speculative possibility. But I am saying that the way the Bible reveals God is at least as important as, if not more important than, our speculative theology in bringing us to know who God is and to know him in a personal relationship—which is what theology ought always to make its first priority.

The Bible tells us that the immutable God has created a temporary, changing world that is real and that in doing so he chose this arena for our existence and for his interactions with us. This observation leads directly to the following chapter.

Before moving on, however, one common response to the kind of tensions expressed in this chapter deserves attention. Theologians are quick to say, "God's immutability does not mean that he cannot act," and they are right. Berkhof observes that it is "customary to speak of God as . . . a God who is always in action."[9] But I would point out that excluding God's actions from the logical implications of immutability is something the theologian decided—even if for good reason. The concept of immutability, in and of itself, does not logically exclude anything. Perhaps, then, when we say God acts, we are again speaking both equivocally and univocally.

---

[9] Berkhof, *Systematic Theology*, 59 (see chap. 1, n. 4). He is clearly wrong, in the same discussion, to say that Arminian doctrine holds "that God is subject to change . . . in His knowledge and will." Arminians hold this no more than Calvinists.

THREE

The Incredible Act of Creation

Implications of the immutability of God, as discussed in the previous chapter, lead directly to this question: How can an eternal, perfectly complete God, needing and desiring nothing he does not already possess, create the changing world of time and space? In that world exist human beings, who are certainly not immutable, acting and deciding things as they go along, and the otherwise immutable God is interacting with them in that journey. How can such a thing be?

This is the age-old philosophical problem of movement and change, considered against the idea of a perfect and immutable God. The theist who thinks logically feels driven to conclude that, for God to be truly immutable, he can never act in any way that he does not act eternally. For him to do something "new," something he has not done forever, seems logically to mean he has changed.

But the fact of creation at least seems to fly squarely in the face of this conclusion. In other words, it appears that the God who cannot act in any way he has not acted eternally created a world that did not exist eternally. This is so incredible that we must explore it in detail.

The Problem of Terminology

Before extended discussion of creation, some preliminary observations about terminology are necessary. In this book I am going to speak of God's creating activity as an act of creation that was not eternal, and I am going to say that God acts in the world of time and space. Using words this way goes against much traditional theological affirmation. The reader needs to understand this and to catch what I mean without being misdirected by the terminology. This requires explanation that is both longer and more technical than I would like for the reader to have to endure.

1. Was God's action in creating eternal? Traditionally, theologians tend to say so. Louis Berkhof, for example, says, "The purpose to create was eternal with Him, and there was no change in Him when this purpose was realized by a single eternal act of His will."[1] This statement may contain some ambiguity, but it appears to affirm that both God's purpose to create and his act that "realized" that purpose were eternal—realized, that is, in the coming-into-existence of the world at the beginning of time. James Dolezal grapples with the issues involved in this tension and concludes that God's creating act is grounded only in his eternal free will, resulting from no necessity within himself or from without. At the same time, he acknowledges the "incomprehensibility" of how God can be, as he is, both "simple" and free to create.[2]

It is common for theologians to say something like this, and their reasons are understandable. To put it simply, they are convinced that an eternal and immutable God cannot logically start (Where in a realm that is eternally the same could something "begin"?) to do something he has not already been doing forever. Paul Helm apparently agrees that someone eternal cannot begin to act.[3]

---

[1] Berkhof, *Systematic Theology*, 59 (see chap. 1, n. 4). Was Berkhof aware how much unresolved tension there is in these words? There is at least as much as in mine!

[2] James E. Dolezal, *God without Parts: Divine Simplicity and the Metaphysics of God's Absoluteness* (Eugene, OR: Pickwick, 2011), 215.

[3] Helm, *Eternal God*, 61 (see chap. 1, n. 5).

This is a logical claim with which one need not disagree. Indeed, the introductory paragraph above says essentially the same thing. Logically speaking, an immutable God cannot do anything he has not done forever. Even so, we are faced with the need to affirm that creation itself is not eternal, and putting these two things together presents a problem both for understanding and for expressing it in words. It would seem clear that in some sense the creating is not an eternal act. I can readily understand an eternal will or purpose or decree to create, but if the act of creating is eternal, it seems logical that what is created is likewise eternal. To create is to activate or cause actual existence, and if God was eternally activating or causing the existence of the world, surely the world was eternally existing. And that conclusion is not acceptable, not for theology or for the biblical account of creation.

Aquinas might have been thinking along similar lines when he carefully worded the statement that "although He had the eternal will to produce some effect, yet He did not produce an eternal effect."[4] Was Aquinas using "produce an effect" to mean the same thing as (but to avoid) my "act to create," as though that solves the problem? Perhaps, perhaps not. Helm quotes the same idea from Aquinas with apparent approval[5] and then quotes Stephen Charnock to say essentially the same thing: "The decree itself was eternal and immutable, but the thing decreed was temporary and mutable."[6]

It's easy to see what's going on here. Aquinas, with others, is drawing some very fine lines—as we theologians (and philosophers) are wont to do. He affirms only that the effect, the created world, is temporal, not that the producing is: God eternally produces a temporal effect, in other words. This has the nicety of avoiding some apparent tensions. But can there be

---

[4] *ST* 1.46.1.

[5] Helm, *Eternal God*, 71, citing Thomas Aquinas, *Summa contra Gentiles*, 2.35.3.

[6] Stephen Charnock, *Discourses upon the Existence and Attributes of God* (1682), 207, cited in Helm, *Eternal God*, 71. Where Charnock has "temporary," we would probably use "temporal."

active producing of an effect without the effect being coextensive with the producing? Even more to the point, is the verb *creating* synonymous with this producing? Could we conform to Aquinas's claim by changing "act of creating" to the simple verb "creating"? That does not seem likely.

Indeed, then, where was the "creating"? Did it take place eternally? Or did it begin when God said, "Let there be light"? Perhaps one will object to the implication of this question on the grounds that the creating of light came straight out of eternity when no time was yet marked, saying that time did not begin until this creating of light took effect. If so, we can rephrase the question to ask whether creating occurred in time when on the second day God said, "Let there be a firmament to divide the waters" (Gen 1:6, paraphrased). Did he create on the second day? What seems clear is that when Gen 1:1 says, "In the beginning God created," the words do not refer to something—whether will or act—"happening" forever in eternity, but to what occurred then and there in the creation account.

I do not mean to be contentious—or naive. No doubt I am more interested in communication than in technical wordings. The wording I use—that God acted to create when he had not done so eternally—should be understood as the same mode of speaking about God that we find in the biblical words "before the foundation of the world," or when we speak of God's eyes. The creation of a world that has not existed forever will still be momentous. The question remains, probably to be answered in the negative, whether we can understand the relationship between eternity and time.[7] The world began to exist when it had not existed eternally, and God

---

[7] Helm, *Eternal God*, 6, acknowledges that for the most part the Bible does not enable us to define God's relationship to time. He agrees that "the idea of timeless eternity is obscure and not fully graspable" (23). For an interesting and highly technical discussion of the relationship between time and eternity, see Leftow, "Eternity and Simultaneity," 148–79 (see chap. 1, n. 6). Among other things, he observes that "there is nothing of God's eternal existence which is 'before' His creating the world: given that He is eternal and has created, He has eternally had the world for company whether or not it is literally present in eternity" (172). Without denying this last affirmation, I am not convinced that it is helpful. Leftow can say it only because he affirms that in God's frame of reference all events in time and space are

caused that existence when he had not caused its existence forever. This is all one needs to understand when I will speak of God's creating as something he had not done eternally.

2. Closely related, can God then act in the world of time and space? No doubt the same fine lines of terminology will apply in answering this question. So long as we affirm the absolute sense of saying that God cannot do anything he has not done eternally, the answer must be negative. But it seems clear that the biblical record intends us to answer the question affirmatively, even if saying so must be taken as both equivocal and univocal.

No doubt traditional theology will say again that the effects of God's acts occur in time and space, not the acts themselves. In this way, what Aquinas said about God's creating can be said about his acting in the created world: "Therefore from the eternal action of God an eternal effect did not follow; but such an effect as God willed, an effect, to wit, which has being after not being."[8]

Consider the creation of Adam on day six, for example, or any other thing created during the creation week. Perhaps some will choose to refer to this action, or any other, as effect rather than act. Helm, for example, offers that if God had an eternal purpose for it to rain today, that purpose is "accomplished" by today's rain.[9] Even so, this wording means the same thing as to say that God acted to bring, or brought, rain today. It is torturous to think we can eliminate active divine agency by the use of the passive verb *accomplished*.

When creating Adam, God made him from the dust of the earth, planted a garden, placed him in it, and spoke several directions to him. That was not done before the sixth day in time, nor was it done in eternity, at least not in the sense meant in the Genesis account of it. When Gen 2:7

---

simultaneous and eternal, while in the world's frame of reference they are temporal and sequential (164, 167–68). Helm, *Eternal God*, 23, denies that "eternity is a kind of simultaneity." I will refer again to the matter of simultaneity.

[8] *ST* 1.46.1.

[9] Helm, *Eternal God*, 63.

says that "the LORD God formed the man out of the dust from the ground and breathed the breath of life into his nostrils," the account, anthropomorphic or not, does not mean he did these things in eternity. Furthermore, we can understand what God did, or does, in eternity only in the terms of what he did in time and space. In other words, in eternity he willed to do exactly what the biblical record represents him as having done and when it represents him as having done it.

When we do theology, we may find ourselves tempted to place such an unbridgeable chasm between God and man that communication and mutual understanding are logically impossible. This may be a tendency of neoorthodoxy or existentialism, for example.[10] It is easy to think of God as so "wholly other" that he cannot speak to us where we are, that even when we speak of him as seeing and hearing, we are expressing truth only as poorest analogy. To such thinking Ps 94:8–10 is a good response; the Lord ridicules senseless people who think he does not see or understand their deeds, asking with strong irony, "Can the one who shaped the ear not hear, / the one who formed the eye not see?" He who made us to bear or be his image, who designed us with the capacity for human language, can he not communicate truth to us in our language? He who created this (objectively existing) time-and-space world, and knows it perfectly, can he not act in it? Or effect a thing or event, if one prefers that language? The idea that God cannot act in our world or communicate with us in our language is simply too ridiculous to affirm.

And if someone should say that at least God could not act in time and space unless he himself was, or became, temporal, a justified response would be: How do you know that?[11] Helm argues that God understands time, including how one event is before or after another, and that this "seems to

---

[10] For a helpful discussion of some of these tendencies, see C. F. H. Henry, "Revelation, Special," in Elwell, ed., *Evangelical Dictionary of Theology*, 945–48 (see chap. 1, n. 6).

[11] Helm, *Eternal God*, 23, correctly affirms that God does not have to be temporal in order to relate to a temporal world.

be implicit in the idea of creation."[12] Surely he is right, and this opens the door to speak of God as acting in time and space.

The Moment of Creation

The previous chapter provides the context for this discussion. There is an eternal state—whether *state* is a good word or not—that only one eternal, unchanging being, God, occupies. His perfect, infinite, eternal existence is that state of being. He has no beginning or end, and nothing else occupies this state with him eternally. He never changes. Saying this expresses what appears to be logically inherent in the concept of immutability.

This brings us, then, to the "moment" of creation—a logical, not a chronological moment, called a moment so we can grasp it. Eternity has no "moments."[13] There is no "before" and "after" within the being of God, no development or becoming taking place. If there is no change, there is neither time nor space.

All Christian theologians (the biblically grounded ones, anyway) will probably agree that the created order is not eternal. Consequently, the creative action of God is in some sense not eternal, as discussed above. Consider again the words of Berkhof: "The purpose to create was eternal with Him, and there was no change in Him when this purpose was realized by a single eternal act of His will." Even if God's purpose to create was eternal, and I am inclined to agree, that does not necessarily mean that God was eternally creating the world.

In actively creating, God does something that he has not done eternally, else the created order would itself—like the eternally begotten Son—be as eternal as he is. In the act of creation, God acted in a way he has not acted forever. But if God can never act in a way he has not acted eternally, for

---

[12] Helm, 24.

[13] Eternity also has no "points." Moments and points are both abstractions and apply only to time and space. Furthermore, in some way beyond the comprehension of most of us (including me), time and space are apparently connected.

him to bring into existence a world that did not exist before seems logically impossible. And yet.

And yet, that is exactly what the unchanging God has done. Whether this seems impossible or not, creation is reality, not an illusion. We are not now figments of God's imagination. Consequently, we may need to take a closer look at our concept of immutability. Perhaps we should say, as we do regarding incorporeality or impassibility, that we speak both equivocally and univocally when we say that God does not change—or does. We need not reexamine the doctrine of creation ex nihilo, but we may need to define immutability more cautiously, at least in such a way that does not insist on all the logical implications of that attribute as human reason sees those logical implications.

God made a world that is not himself. Christian theology is not pantheism. The cosmos had a beginning. God spoke it into existence, and it is not identical to him or part of him. The Bible speaks of what was true "before the foundation of the world" (Eph 1:4; 1 Pet 1:20), and it is logically impossible for there to be a "before" for an eternal, unchanging God. But the language is both biblical and appropriate—even if relational.[14] Perhaps, then, to us such language is anthropomorphic, the only way we can conceive the noneternal creative act of an eternally unchanging God.

To speak of something as happening "before the foundation of the world" is apparently to speak relationally. Whatever this means—even if we give up on explaining what it means—the revealed truth remains: the eternally perfect and fully self-satisfied God "actualized" a world that did not exist before that moment, the moment when our time and space world began.

An incredible thing transpired. Something new began, something not coeternal with an eternal, unchanging God. Unbelievable or not, we believe it. The Bible affirms it. We bow in adoration and submission to him.

---

[14] It may be helpful to think of "before" as "logically," not "temporally" antecedent. Perhaps the truth in this should be regarded as primarily conceptual, emphasizing that God himself is "before"—founder—of the world. The world is not self-creating but exists only in complete dependence on him.

God in a New Relationship?

Having acted to bring into existence a world that did not exist before, God thus brought about a relationship for himself that he did not have eternally—or "previously," as impossible as that adverb is.[15] The Scriptures report that he upholds or sustains the created order by his powerful word (Heb 1:3; Col 1:17). He was not doing that "before," not forever.[16]

Furthermore, this new situation for God involves a personal relationship with the human beings he created in his image. His own word for us is that he loves us. The words of Psalm 8 leave us in no doubt: he is mindful of us, he visits us. He is providentially active to work all things together for the good of those whom he has lovingly acknowledged as his own (Rom 8:28). He has not been arranging things this way eternally.

So, the God who is immutable has created a world that did not exist before. He has a relationship with it that did not exist before.[17] This is so incredible that repetition is unavoidable. This new existence and

---

[15] The idea of God's "relations" is debated in theology, including issues about his "essential relations." My wording is not meant to speak to such issues, only to express some important "relational" considerations.

[16] An editor has suggested that this sounds similar to the view of Jay Wesley Richards, *The Untamed God: A Philosophical Exploration of Divine Perfection, Simplicity and Immutability* (Downers Grove, IL: InterVarsity, 2003), who distinguishes between God's essential, unchanging properties and his "contingent properties" involved in how he relates to what is not him. I am not attempting anything so intricate as that. For his view and James Dolezal's critique and disagreement, see Dolezal's *God without Parts*, esp. pp. 194–97.

[17] Thanks to Steven Lewis for pointing me to Thomas Aquinas's use of "real relation" and "relation of reason" in discussing God's relation to the world. See *ST* 1.13.7 for Thomas's denial that God has a "real relation" to the created world. This philosophical distinction is highly technical and does not affect the point I am making; indeed, Aquinas affirmed a "relation of reason" between God and the world, and, as Earl Muller observes, even a logical or rational relationship is "still true" (678). See Earl Muller, "Real Relations and the Divine: Issues in Thomas's Understanding of God's Relation to the World," *Theological Studies* 56 (1995): 673–95. Helm, *Eternal God*, 24, affirms that God has "positive" or "real relations" with creation and with individuals in time.

relationship seem logically impossible for an absolutely immutable, eternal being. A perfectly self-satisfied God—who cannot desire or need anything other than himself and to whose completeness nothing can be added—logically cannot act or experience anything he has not acted or experienced forever. As Kenneth Keathley observes, God's "act of creation was completely gratuitous."[18] God did not need to create, much less have to. Logically, then, it would seem that he cannot possibly create a world that did not eternally coexist with him. He cannot make beings who act. He cannot love them. He cannot interact with them.

How wonderfully incredible, then! That is exactly what he has done. I am driven to the conclusion, therefore, that the problem lies in our finite, human logic. And by the same impulse I am driven to awe and worship, to exclaim with Paul, "How unsearchable his judgments / and untraceable his ways!" (Rom 11:33). I am tempted to cite yet another of the attributes traditionally ascribed to God: he is inscrutable.

Perhaps we must forgo explanation and resort to mystery, to what is beyond human comprehension. Perhaps our logic is not quite up to the task of comprehending the infinite God or his attributes.[19]

Two Justified Implications

Describing God—speaking about him—remains at least partly beyond the limits of our language and logic. Even so, at least two helpful implications exist of the incredible fact that the eternal, immutable God has created the world of time and space.

---

[18] Kenneth Keathley, *Salvation and Sovereignty: A Molinist Approach* (Nashville: B&H Academic, 2019), 26.

[19] Such reading as I have done on this subject leads me to conclude that the difference between my view and that of others is that they choose to resolve the tension by affirming that from the perspective of God in eternity his creating is eternal although the world he is creating is not. I, on the other hand, am content to leave the tension unresolved and affirm both God's immutability and that he was not actively creating the world eternally.

The first is this: When we attribute to God certain qualities of essence, we should realize that not all the conclusions that can be logically derived from those qualities may be justified.[20] This is especially true when our logical inferences appear to be in conflict with what the Bible actually affirms about God. As discussed in chapter 1, we may attribute incorporeality to God, but the Bible straightforwardly speaks of his body parts. Yes, that manner of speaking is anthropomorphic, but we had better not say this as a way of pushing aside the truth involved in what the Bible says.

Likewise, if we affirm that God is impassible, and inspired Scripture tells us that God feels things, it is probably more important for us to question our understanding of impassibility than for us to question the biblical affirmations. In other words, when we try to define too closely the nature of the infinite God and his attributes, considered apart from the biblical account, our logic is not fully dependable. Understanding infinite impassibility may be a step beyond the minds and reasoning of finite beings.

The same is true for God's immutability. If what the Bible reports about God's creative acts has the appearance of being in some ways in tension with any logical implications we draw from immutability, it is the latter—the logical implications we draw—that we should question rather than the more or less obvious meaning of Scripture.[21] The Bible tells us forthrightly that God has acted to create a world in which other beings act in time and space and he interacts with them. That understanding is too important to be mitigated by a priori, metaphysical, theological constructs about God or his eternal will and purposes.

The second implication has other ideas inherent within it. The incredible act of God to create the space–time cosmos with human beings in it—which is only apparently impossible for an eternally unchanging God—means that

---

[20] Those who emphasize that our speech about God is analogical may tend to say that this tension results from that fact. They may be right.

[21] By no means do I intend to abandon or even to cast suspicion on God's immutability itself.

we live in the real world that God created, and in our world God interacts with us, and this is the primary subject matter of the Bible.

Philosophers of time discuss at great length whether God is timeless or temporal.[22] Some of their logic is difficult to follow, and perhaps they need to consider that their words may be both equivocal and univocal. What is more certain is saying that the biblical record makes clear, almost by definition, that God acts in the real time-and-space world he created and in the ways depicted in that record—regardless of what fine lines are drawn by choosing intricate terminology to skirt or qualify this truth.

Drawing some further conclusions will emphasize the importance of this point. The clear implication of this discussion is that this world of time and space—the world that makes up the primary story of the Bible—is of paramount importance. That God spoke this world into existence and fashioned us to bear or be his likeness and placed us in it and upholds all things and interacts with us in this world, as the biblical narrative describes, is incredible for an immutable God. And the significance of this creative work of God's is altogether essential for us to understand him or ourselves or what transpires between him and us.

Creating this world means that God chose to make this world the arena in which we act and in which he interacts with us. This is the realm in which God has chosen to act, and that fact fills it with meaning. Whether it is logically possible for an eternal and unchanging God to act at all, or to act in ways he has not acted forever, we may not know for sure, but there is enough tension there for us to say that his creative acts are momentous. That he created this world is so important that the meaning of this action must bear on every aspect of our theology.

---

[22] See, for example, William Lane Craig, *Time and Eternity: Exploring God's Relationship to Time* (Wheaton: Crossway, 2001), who contends that the timeless God became temporal at creation. See also Davis, *Logic and the Nature of God*, 8–24, esp. 22 (see chap. 2, n. 4), who considers whether God is timelessly or temporally eternal and argues for the latter.

Here in this world, which he apparently found so important to create—and to say this may be highly presumptuous—is the arena or domain in which he has determined to act. Whatever he has "done" in eternity—whatever plan he has instituted or decisions he has made or whatever he knows forever—he acts in the world of time and space. And all his eternal willings and purposes find their meaning in these acts. We know what God is and knows in eternity by what he has done in time and space, and we have the divinely inspired revelation of what he has done to inform us.

In Shakespeare's *As You Like It*, the character Jacques says, "All the world's a stage, and all the men and women merely players."[23] Whether a stage or a play is the best metaphor is questionable, but Jacques is right. And he would have been equally right to add that God himself has chosen to create this "stage" on which he likewise takes an all-important role. This is the real world, and the actions of God and human beings in it are their real actions.

Think of it! Out of an infinitely perfect, eternal, unchanging existence God chose to bring into existence a changing world populated with all sorts of wonderful things. The most wonderful of all? Beings who reflect his image and with whom he interacts on a personal level. The story of that world and their interactions is the subject of the Bible.

I cannot imagine what prompted God to do that.[24] Nothing outside himself, of course. There was nothing outside himself. Regardless, his creation of this world must mean something special. This space–time world is important to him. This is the domain where he acts to implement his plan, not in unchanging eternity.

---

[23] William Shakespeare, *As You Like It*, act 2, scene 7, line 138.

[24] Helm, *Eternal God*, 171, suggests that a self-sufficient God creates out of his "overflowing goodness," not from his own need. Aquinas (*ST* 1.28.1) observed that God "does not produce the creature by necessity of His nature." He also says (*ST* 1.46.1) that "things are necessary, according as it is necessary for God to will them," and yet that it is not necessary for the world "to be *always*" (i.e., exist eternally).

The Reality of This World

For background, I need to reference my personal experience. In my very first philosophy class long ago, I was introduced to one of the persistent questions of philosophy: What sort of stuff makes up this world? Among others, there are three basic metaphysical answers to the question. Some say that everything that exists is matter—whatever "matter" is. This view is materialism or naturalism, and I will assume without argument that this cannot be a truly Christian, biblical worldview. Others say that only minds and/or ideas exist, although there are many forms of idealism, which need no explanation here. I assume that idealism, in some form, can be consonant with the biblical account of things. Still others hold to dualism, insisting that both mind and matter are ultimately real. Some version of this, too, can be a Christian worldview.[25]

I myself was somewhat attracted to personal idealism. I am not entirely committed, but I am open to the possibility that the atoms of physical stuff are ultimately mental and personal, that subatomic particles have the nature of energy, and that this energy is that of a mind at work. I hasten to acknowledge that most people probably will not want to think of sticks and rainbows that way and will prefer to be (qualified) dualists.

Regardless, in that class I became acquainted with the view of George Berkeley (1685–1753), bishop of the Church of England and a philosophical idealist. Berkeley said, "*Esse est percipi*" ("To be is to be perceived"). For him, the physical world we live in is apparently pure perception, as experienced by persons. In time, I decided that his philosophy, though conceiving of God biblically in many respects, did not conceive of creation biblically. I tend to think that to do justice to the biblical account of creation, one must affirm the reality of the physical world in time and space—whatever the ultimate nature of the stuff the world is made of. When God spoke this

---

[25] Warren C. Young, *A Christian Approach to Philosophy* (Grand Rapids: Baker, 1954), held that "contingent dualism" is the best expression of a Christian worldview. But I suspect that to speak of "contingent" reality is to beg the question of ultimate reality.

cosmos into existence, placed us in it, and chose to interact with us in it, that incredible act gave status to this realm. This world is reality. God made it and is active in it.

I am not suggesting that anyone who believes the Bible would deny this last affirmation. I am saying, however, that this world and its events—and the Bible contains the story of our existence and God's interaction with us in this world—mean just what the Bible presents them as meaning and therefore what the eternal God intended them to mean. This needs emphasizing over against some theologians who become so occupied with what God is in himself forever, and with his eternal attributes and knowledge and decrees, that those concepts threaten to devour the truth about this world and its story contained in the Bible and experienced by us.

This danger arises when things that are part of life, in time and space, have to be qualified so much—to comport with an a priori concept of God in eternity—that we cannot believe persons and events are what they present themselves as being. And I do not merely, or even primarily, mean what they seem to be in our experience. I mean what they seem to be in the biblical record primarily and in our experience that is in accord with that record.

Perhaps, then, we should begin with the world we live in, and our history in that world as presented in Scripture, and then acknowledge that some of the logical implications of our theological constructs must be held cautiously.[26] If we conceive of God's immutability in too rational and absolute a fashion, we make the act of creation incoherent. That is the reason for starting with creation, understanding immutability and other aspects of God's being like his purposes and knowledge in light of the biblical account of the real world. After all, that is where the Bible starts: "In the beginning, God created . . ." Our discussion should focus on the

---

[26] The reader will understand, I trust, that I am not advocating the abandonment of theological constructs as such, not even those framed in philosophical terminology. Many important truths are expressed in theological constructs. However, they must be evaluated, if not qualified, by what the Bible says or implies about the truths they aim to define.

reality of this world and of God's creation of it and interaction with it as described in the Bible.

The doctrine of creation ex nihilo, presumably, needs no defense, at least not among traditional theologians. While process theologians think otherwise, all Bible-believing theologians will agree that God spoke the created order into existence when it was not "there" before. It did not exist eternally. It came into existence "in the beginning." And in saying this much we speak more univocally than equivocally.

Then God's immutability cannot be allowed to mitigate that fact—if anyone is tempted along those lines. If we conceive of immutability in a way that diminishes the meaning of this sudden, radical, momentous creation, we must modify our concept of immutability, not our view of the reality of the created order. The meaning of this fact seems clear, then. What we perceive as taking place in this world of time and space is real, at least in all the respects that are confirmed in Scripture.

The Bible does not undertake to describe God for us, before the present cosmos, at least not primarily. To be sure, the Bible includes affirmations here and there about God that reach back into his eternal state, as in that great "prayer of Moses the man of God": "Before . . . you gave birth to the earth and the world, / from eternity to eternity, you are God" (Ps 90:2). For the most part, however, the Bible is about God in his relationship to the created world. The narrative, from Genesis to Revelation, is about God and man and the world and how they interact. And in understanding this we derive a theology of God's purposes and knowledge. What he has done and how he has done it in time and space are exactly what reveals his eternal purposes and knowledge.

This is so important for the purpose of this work that I will spend more than one chapter discussing specific biblical passages and how we should read them in light of the reality of this world. First, however, I have one more chapter treating a matter of huge importance, as important as creation itself, for affirming the reality of this world and of God's interaction with us in this world.

FOUR

The Incarnation of God

Something else God did is just as incredible as creation, something that demonstrates beyond question that he has chosen this world to be the arena in which he acts. This momentous something is the incarnation of the Second Person of the triune Godhead, which shows without doubt that (1) God is "involved" with us in this world, and (2) he has entered into a relationship with us that he did not have eternally.

Indeed, the Bible says something that would appear to affirm a metaphysical change in the Deity, and it goes well beyond the implications of the preceding chapter. At the very least, the inspired writer, reflecting the Divine Author overshadowing him, apparently sensed no conflict with the doctrine of immutability in his matter-of-fact affirmation.

I am referring to the first chapter of the Gospel of John. In the first verses of the chapter, John has expressed the amazing truth about creation, reaching back to the beginning: "In the beginning was the Word, . . . and the Word was God" (v. 1).

Then: "All things were created through him" (v. 3). John is unabashed. This Logos, this Second Person of the Trinity, is the creating God of Genesis 1.

As the Word of God, he is God's speaking, "Let there be light"—and so on. This, too, is stunning.

And then an even more startling thing: "The Word became flesh and dwelt among us. We observed his glory" (v. 14). The Word became flesh![1] The Greek verb (*ginomai*) apparently means becoming something that was not already so. Indeed, the Arndt-Gingrich lexicon, in its article on this verb, includes this verse in the section illustrating the meaning: "of pers. and things *which change their nature*, to indicate their entering a new condition."[2]

That meaning, applied to the Logos, does not sound very much like divine immutability, and it begets a measure of uncertainty as to how to express the nature of the incarnation. On the one hand, John 1:14 need not mean that there was a change in the nature of God or that God became someone or something he was not already. On the other hand, John was certainly not being careful to avoid giving such an impression. Under the Spirit's superintendence he said that God the eternal Logos became flesh, when he was not flesh before. As discussed earlier with regard to creation, one may say that the act of becoming incarnate was eternal but its effect was temporal, but that simply does not seem to do justice to the inspired record.

Something incredible happened in the incarnation. An eternal, unchanging God became one of us. At least, one of the three persons in the Godhead did so—and to be able to separate the persons this way is even more a mystery. To try to explain this is painful. Such an incarnation seems as impossible, logically, as creation itself (the previous chapter). The God who is pure being with no hint of becoming, the God who has existed

---

[1] "The Logos *became* flesh—not merely entered into, clothed himself with . . . not merely appeared as . . . but became flesh"—James Dunn, *Christology in the Making* (Louisville: Westminster, 1980), 240, cited in Helm, *Eternal God*, 7 (see chap. 1, n. 5).

[2] William F. Arndt and E. Wilbur Gingrich, *A Greek-English Lexicon of the New Testament and Other Early Christian Literature* (Chicago: University of Chicago, 1957), 158 (emphasis added).

forever in infinite perfection, eternally everything he can be with no potential to become anything else, has become what he was not before.[3]

Explaining this event seems beyond anyone's ability. We can affirm it, in faith, believing it because God has revealed it to us. Then, once accepting it as true, we can build theological-logical constructs that attempt to define the incarnate Logos, the person Jesus Christ. One person, two natures, we say. Truly God in every respect, as much so as if he had not become incarnate. Truly human in every respect, as much so as if he were the natural son of Joseph and Mary but without a sinful nature. And we must not, we remind ourselves, divide the person or mingle the natures.

Such a construct is puny—as are all our attempts to explain God, especially when we reach beyond what the Bible itself says. Puny, yes, but the best we can do and important to affirm. In the end we know that the incredible incarnation is reality. Jesus Christ is Immanuel, God with us, God one of us. This truth remains a mystery, beyond the limitations of our ability to comprehend or define. An eternal, unchanging God cannot become a human being. Yet that is exactly what he did.

Some interpreters attempt to mitigate this by affirming that the incarnation did not represent change but only represented the addition of a human nature to the eternal, divine nature of the Logos. Shedd opines: "The Divine essence . . . assumed a human nature into union with himself."[4] Yes, but logically this solves nothing. A being that is already everything he can be cannot possibly add, or assume, anything to himself. Berkhof insists, "The incarnation brought no change in the Being or perfections of God, nor in His purpose, for it was His eternal good pleasure to send the Son of His love into the world."[5] He is right, but the words only gloss over the tension. God's purpose was eternal; the incarnation was not.

---

[3] I assume that those who say God was creating the world eternally, from the vantage point of his frame of reference, would say the same about the incarnation. Saying this about either is equally difficult to comprehend.

[4] Shedd, *Dogmatic Theology*, 1:359 (see chap. 2, n. 6).

[5] Berkhof, *Systematic Theology*, 59 (see chap. 1, n. 4).

As incomprehensible as the incarnation is, however, some of its implications are clear, including what the previous chapters affirm about the implications of creation. The incarnation makes clearer than anything except creation itself that God acts within the space–time world he created. Could anything be clearer than the words of the inspired apostle: "When the time came to completion, God sent his Son, born of a woman" (Gal 4:4)? These words make the point dramatically: God acted in time—at the choicest moment of time—and the incarnation exquisitely instructs us thus.

The previous chapter expressed the fact that God has obviously chosen to make this world the arena in which he acts. The incarnation is irrefutable evidence of this fact. It proves beyond doubt that God is aware of what is going on in the world as it is going on. That he knows (even better than we) the implications of time and movement in the course of history. That he is entirely capable of taking a hand in earth's affairs. That he acts, and interacts with us, in time and space.

To put this another way, the incarnation did not take place in eternity, and even if it did in some sense, the Bible is not referring to that. Furthermore, if we cannot say that there was a time before creation, as we technically cannot, there most certainly was a time before the incarnation—several thousand years of time, at least. John 1:14 anchors the incarnation in time and space: "The Word became flesh *and dwelt [tabernacled] among us*" (emphasis added). The incarnation took place at a specific time and place in the history of the world. The Word became flesh "in the days of King Herod of Judea" (Luke 1:5), on a certain date—around 6 BC—on the calendar. It took place in Nazareth when a pure young woman named Mary, betrothed to Joseph, was visited by the Spirit of God, who "overshadowed" her and supernaturally ignited life in the egg in her womb—and not mere life, but divine life. I repeat that this action was not in eternity; it was in the sixth month of the pregnancy of Elizabeth, wife of Zechariah (Luke 1:26, 35). If we knew everything we wish we knew, we could pinpoint the exact date and place. We are sure there was an exact date and place.

This does not imply that there was no plan for the incarnation in the mind of God in eternity. Surely there was. But this is to say that, whatever that eternal plan was, its context was in the world that would be in time and space. In eternity God planned to become incarnate in 6 BC, if that was the date. We grasp the eternal knowledge and purpose as being exactly what is recorded as taking place in time.

We may not understand everything that is involved in this relationship between eternity and time—and subsequent chapters will devote considerable discussion to this matter. But whatever the relationship is, it is the incarnation in time and space that is the reality, that matters, and that John 1:14 is describing. The incarnation was not a fact until that date during the reign of Herod and that place in Nazareth where the angel visited Mary. That is when God acted, not before. That is when the incarnation took place. That is when the Word became flesh, when the Logos became a human being. The eternal Logos was not the God-man; he did not possess a human nature in eternity. Apparently he does now.

Some may say that this discussion is pedantic, that of course everyone knows this to be true. Perhaps, but not everyone keeps it in the proper perspective when we discuss the eternal decrees and knowledge of God. It is important for us to see the events in the biblical record as the key to conceiving of God and his eternal attributes and knowledge and purposes. The next two chapters will illustrate this principle with more biblical examples.

FIVE

Reading the Bible: Examples of God at Work in This World (Part I)

The previous chapters focus on the momentous importance of creation. The eternal, infinite, immutable God, against anything expected, has brought into existence a world other than himself and placed in it human beings expressing—perhaps "reflecting" is a better word—his image. For reasons best known to himself, he has chosen to make this world the arena for his actions, including his providential management of our affairs from day to day in his interaction with us. This, then, is the real world; it is "where the action is." God acts in time and space with us, not in eternity.[1]

The incarnation is an equally significant example of God's acting in time and space. In this chapter and the next, I will pursue a number of

---

[1] I do not mean to offend by adding "not in eternity." I will not keep saying so, but I most certainly believe God has willed his actions in eternity. The acts themselves—including the incarnation discussed in the previous chapter and those dealt with in these chapters—take place in time and space, and there their meaning is revealed.

biblical examples of divine interaction with us in this world and will make observations that focus on the real meaning of that interaction.

The examples in this chapter will treat matters that have a larger biblical focus. Those in the next chapter will be about more specific incidents that speak especially to contingencies and God's foreknowledge, leading to the second major part of this book.

1. Creation and the Fall in Genesis 1–3

I have already dealt with the act of creation as such. I choose now to focus on some of the details, on God's creative activity as described in the opening chapters of Genesis. Without getting embroiled in an old debate, I say simply that I read the creation account as having historical meaning rather than being mere parable. Even so, most of those who regard the account as suprahistorical in some way will probably acknowledge that there was a beginning of things that did not exist before.[2]

The Genesis record speaks of a "beginning." It affirms that God spoke into existence, or commanded to exist, things that did not exist before. Psalm 33 is just one of many biblical confirmations: "The heavens were made by the word of the LORD, / and all the stars, by the breath of his mouth" (v. 6). "For he spoke, and it [the earth] came into being; / he commanded, and it came into existence" (v. 9). See also Heb 11:3 and 2 Pet 3:5.

Significantly, Genesis frames these creative acts in time and gives them order: the light-bearers—sun, moon, and stars—on the fourth day, for example, directly across from the first day when he said, "Let there be light."

---

[2] Without straying too far from my purpose, I observe that there is a radical difference, as to the story of humanity, between the biblical-Christian worldview and that of secular science. The latter emphasizes continuity with an almost infinite past, while the Bible views the creation of the cosmos and mankind as a new work of God that serves as a beginning. When science assumes that there is no supernatural, it dooms itself to be wrong. As Steven Lewis, on reading this, observed, "Science goes well beyond its purview if it makes any claim whatsoever about anything beyond the natural world—even to deny its existence."

On the sixth day he created human beings, likewise corresponding to the third day when he gave definition to the waters and the land masses to provide a domain for human beings and a wide variety of animals.

There is no need here to argue when that was: certainly not in 4004 BC, as Archbishop Ussher calculated. Young earth versus old earth? The answer does not matter for what I am saying here. On the one hand, I am satisfied that the Bible does not enable us to say just when God's week of creation was. And I am just as confident that the biblical account does not require millions of years for creation, since if God ever brought into existence any things that did not exist before, bare science—by definition—cannot determine how old they are. Whatever God made, whether oak tree or acorn, he made in a state of being that must otherwise reflect a prior state.

None of that is important for the discussion here. What is important is that there was a when, and it was as real as today's date. In creating what did not exist eternally, God started time and space. There the Bible begins, and from then on the narrative is about God's interaction with humanity and the created order.

Without continuing this discussion at great length, I will take it on as far as the fall. God dealt with Adam and Eve, the original pair, in the time and places indicated in the Genesis narrative. He created them from the soil and put them in a place where there was food. He warned them that if they ate from the tree forbidden them they would die at that very time. And when they ate, he came to them and confronted them then and there, pronouncing judgment and excluding them from the garden they had tended before. None of that happened before; the record does not set the event in eternity, it does not even reference anything that happened in eternity. Adam and Eve sinned in real time. God sought them out and judged them after they sinned, not before. Any interpretation of God's plans for the fall made in eternity—his decrees, in other words—ought to be understood as plans for the fall to be exactly as it is portrayed in the Genesis record, a plan that included the fact that they would freely disobey when they could have obeyed.

Again, the account speaks as historical narrative, and reading it as some sort of metanarrative should not finally change the main truths. Unless God created humanity as sinful, there was a time when humanity's situation changed—from innocence to depravity, from being spiritually alive to being spiritually dead. Whatever all this means, human beings were relocated outside the garden and could not go back. These things transpired in time and space under the hand of the God who created them in his image and tested their loyalty to him.

The crucial question is why God chose to create a world in which those he made to bear or be his image would sin and bring evil into that world. He has not revealed the answer, and our logic is not sufficient for us to derive one.

The point, regardless, is that he did create the world in which evil would arise, and it did. It would not have come had he not created human beings, and in his omniscience he knew they would sin. But he did not cause the sin, not in any sense of the word *cause*.[3] That he created us knowing we would do this does not make him the cause.[4] For a poor example of the relationship, if I were to give my child unconditional freedom to choose whether to have pizza or spinach for dinner, I would not thereby be the cause of either choice, even though I created the situation in which the choice is made. Choices are self-determined.

The crucial event was that human beings were free to choose for or against God, and they could have chosen for him and did not. Nothing in the record suggests that Adam and Eve had to sin; we are not supposed to think that. They—we—are the cause of sin, which began when we, in our dependence, acted independently of, and so in disobedience to, our

---

[3] I am aware that philosophers and theologians make distinctions between senses of the word *cause*, including the difference between formal, final, efficient, and material causes. Properly understood, at least one of these might be used for the relationship between God and sin. But I would contend that some word other than *cause* should be found; the church and the world in general will misunderstand if we say (whatever we mean) that God is the "cause" of sin. I am inclined, on this point, to agree with the Canons of Dort, Article 15, which said that "the notion that God is the author of sin in any way 'at all' is 'a blasphemous thought.'" Keathley, *Salvation and Sovereignty*, 144 (see chap. 3, n. 18).

[4] See Robert E. Picirilli, *Free Will Revisited: A Respectful Response to Luther, Calvin, and Edwards* (Eugene, OR: Wipf & Stock, 2017), esp. 105–9.

Creator. Sin is not physical or external; it exists only in the motives and wills of human beings.[5]

To return to what is important for the present discussion, the fall did not happen in eternity. It happened then, when they sinned, and it happened there, in Eden. Adam and Eve sinned then, and God enacted their punishment then. And the rest of the human story flows from that.

In summary, Scripture presents the fall to us as real history, in the world of time and space we inhabit. God willed and acted, setting alternatives before those he had created. They willed and acted, choosing between those alternatives when either choice was possible. God responded as he had said he would, ushering in justice and offering grace. That is where the action—the interaction—was, not in some other realm, not in eternity. The nature of the events can straightforwardly be understood from the way the biblical account presents them. The meaning is to be found there, and any eternal plan of the Creator should be expressed in accord with that meaning.

God is unchanging. But time and space and human beings are not, and God knows just how to interact with the created order in its constant change without himself being subject to change in his essence or nature. For us, as for Adam and Eve, the world we inhabit is real, and God is in it with us. The drama has not already played out, with this world being some hollow, Platonic reflection of an eternal reality. This is the world God created for the divine-human drama, and we should take it seriously.

2. Deuteronomy 30 and the Choices God Offers

In the Bible, God often sets choices before human beings. Of many possible examples of this, one of the most telling appears in Moses's farewell speeches to Israel, as in Deut 30:11–20: "See, today I have set before you life and

---

[5] That God actualized this world (with its sin) out of all possible worlds makes him responsible for the world that includes sin. He is responsible for the possibility of sin. But he is not responsible for the sin itself.

prosperity, death and adversity" (v. 15). The Lord said, "I have set before you life and death, blessing and curse. Choose life" (v. 19).[6]

It seems obvious that for the Lord to "set before" people two options means that he offers options that are really possible, even if his gracious work is required to enable a positive choice. A passage like this is an invitation, not merely a setting forth of God's law to remind people that they are unable to obey him, as Luther and Calvin interpreted it. It is a gracious invitation, in that the spoken word and the accompanying work of God's Spirit to give understanding and persuade, serve to enable depraved persons, otherwise unable to choose for God, to respond favorably to the invitation while retaining the power to resist.

This is the way the passage presents itself to us. Indeed, this is the way the inspired apostle interprets it in Rom 10:6–10, applying Moses's words to the all-important interaction involved in gospel salvation. For that matter, Paul says that the word Moses gave is in fact the "message of faith that we proclaim" (v. 8)—the gospel, in other words. For Paul "the righteousness that comes from faith" (v. 6) was speaking in Deuteronomy.

Moses himself said, as Paul notes, that what was asked of the Israelites was not far removed from them or out of reach (Deut 30:11–14). In other words, the gracious offer of faith was truly possible for them, in spite of their depravity, made possible by the powerful word of God as brought to their understanding by the Spirit of God.

Then the Lord, through Moses, was setting before them "live" options in space and time. There is no need to read into this a darker implication that the only thing truly available to them was hopeless despair because they could not respond positively. And if someone should say that they could cast

---

[6] For a more complete treatment of this passage, see Picirilli, *Free Will Revisited*, 26–29. As discussed there, a relatively uncommon construction appears in Deuteronomy 30, translated "I have set before you," followed by options. Other than in that chapter, the specific construction occurs again only in Deut 11:26 and in Jer 21:8, where the Lord set before the inhabitants of Jerusalem, under siege, the options of surrendering to the Babylonians and surviving or of resisting and perishing. Surely the intended meaning is that they could choose either course.

themselves on God for mercy, that is exactly what I am saying. Nothing in the text suggests that the whole outcome had already been predetermined by God in eternity, making just one choice possible in the circumstances. The drama was being played out in time, not in eternity. Both God and human beings were exerting influence and deciding responses, then and there.

Similar invitations in our day are likewise in time and space, inviting us to choose for God or against him here and now. Furthermore, God's foreknowledge and eternal plan do not serve to transfer such events in human history backward into eternity.[7] Those events happen only as they happen in this world, and with the meaning that applies at the time, including the full implications of any contingencies—alternative choices—that are involved. In Deuteronomy 30, the people could have chosen life or death. No doubt some, with the enabling of the Spirit, chose the one, and some, resisting that same enabling, chose the other.

3. Psalms Recounting God's Dealings with Israel in History

The biblical descriptions of God's actions in human history speak to us in the same voice. Any number of passages could be cited here. Psalm 78 is striking in its appropriateness for this point. It is a dramatic description of God's actions in Israel's history, following the psalmist's opening remarks (vv. 1–8) about the importance of this history for future generations. Indeed, history's failures make valuable instruction.

Israel forgot the works of God, the "wondrous works" he had displayed in Egypt (vv. 9–11). These works included dividing the Red Sea (vv. 12–13), leading them through the wilderness by a cloud or pillar of fire (v. 14),

---

[7] I realize that no one would say such a thing. But when we burden present-time events with a preformed view of God's decrees as controlling them, we are in effect making such a transfer. Instead, we should read into God's decrees exactly what biblical events are revealed to mean, including when those events involve free, self-determined choices. If we read the history correctly, we do not need to read more into the decrees.

and giving them abundance of water from rock (vv. 15–16). Even so, they sinned grievously, questioning God, and he became "furious" with them because of their unbelief in the face of what he had provided (vv. 17–25). So, he demonstrated his power by bringing in quail to satisfy their craving. Then, while they gorged, his wrath arose and he slew the very stoutest of them (vv. 26–31). For all this they were unrepentant, and he consumed their days in futility in the wilderness (vv. 32–33).

The psalm continues along these lines, rehearsing the history, moving from Israel's bondage in Egypt all the way to the time of David. Even when Israel seemed to seek God, they only flattered him; even so, in his compassion he forgave them time and again, forgoing their destruction and turning away from his anger (vv. 34–39). Repeatedly they provoked him, ignoring the mighty acts he had performed in rescuing them from their bondage—which they had observed—including his angry destruction of the Egyptians (vv. 40–53). Still, although he finally brought them into Canaan and established them there in safety, they were unfaithful and provoked him again to wrath with their high places and idols (vv. 54–58). This led to astounding acts of God: he "heard"; he "became furious"; he "abandoned" his earthly dwelling place; he gave them up into captivity; he "surrendered" them to the sword (vv. 59–64). Afterward, he "awoke" and "beat back" his foes and "chose" Judah and David as agents of his redemptive purpose for them (vv. 65–72).

To focus on the big picture rather than dwelling on details reveals the telling drama that the psalmist recounts. What he describes here is real history, the actions of humans and God within history. This is where the action is, this is when and where God did the things described in the verbs of action emphasized above.

Probably no one will directly disagree with what I have just said, but determinists may not focus on this narrative as they ought. They will say, instead, that God did these things in eternity. However, what the record describes did not occur in eternity. Although God was eternally aware of this history and of his plan of action in it, he did not do any of this until the time of the exodus from Egypt and wilderness wanderings and conquest of

Canaan and anointing of David.[8] The events narrated here were not some mere replaying of a movie God had already watched. Whatever he knew and purposed in eternity was to do exactly what the record indicates he did in response to the free acts of human beings. He had not already "settled" all this, by means of his eternal decrees, in a way that made it all necessary and predetermined.

These things happened only when and where the biblical narrative describes them as happening: in the world of time and space in whatever years BC they occurred. Not until then did Israel forget God's power and taunt him with the question of whether he could provide them meat to eat. Not until then did the Lord hear their expression of lack of faith and become furious. Not until they were eating the quail did the Lord's wrath provoke him to slay those who were "stout" in their challenge to him. Not until they tempted and provoked God with their high places and carved images did he become furious again and forsake them and deliver them into captivity and slaughter.

There are many other passages that present the very same perspective on the history of Israel and God's acts toward them. Psalms 105 and 106 say many things very similar to the things just cited. Psalm 106 includes especially dramatic description of the back-and-forth, influence-and-response actions of Israel and Yahweh: They rebelled by the Red Sea (v. 7); nevertheless he saved them (v. 8). They, on their part, believed and sang his praises (v. 12); they soon forgot and tested him (vv. 13–14). He, on his part, acceded to their request but sent a "wasting disease among them" (v. 15)—and so on. Especially significant, he said he would destroy them, but Moses interceded and turned aside Yahweh's wrath (v. 23).[9] Likewise telling are vv. 44–45: God heard their cry and had regard for their

---

[8] One should not take me to mean that God is temporal—an issue I will touch on in a subsequent chapter. But he is fully capable of acting in time, and the biblical account tells about his acts in time.

[9] This verse refers to Exodus 32, a passage I will address in a subsequent chapter on theology in Exodus.

circumstances, remembered his covenant, and relented in accord with the multitude of his mercies.

In all this narrative, human action in history brings divine response, likewise in history. In one sense, nothing else matters but that. If, as a result of our a priori concepts of God in eternity, we make the story mean something different from that, we have distorted the account.

By no means am I denying that God, in eternity, foresaw all this perfectly and knew exactly how to incorporate it all into his plan. But whatever he knew in eternity, he knew only from its taking place in time and space and from his purposes that events take place as observed in history.[10] All the blessings and curses he willed in eternity he willed in response to the occurrences in time and space. One who misses that relationship misses everything. If one sees the meaning of the events in history as secondary to or controlled or caused by God's eternal purposes, one has turned reality on its head. Instead, it is the events of history that are primary and expose and explain God's eternal decrees.

If that were not so, I suggest that the infinite and immutable God would not have created the world of time and space.

4. Passages Depicting God's Decisions in Time

Examples closely related to the preceding are passages that represent God as making decisions in time. Among many of these is Psalm 95, which also looks back on Israel's history following the exodus from Egypt.

The psalmist invites his hearers (thinking orally) to hearken to God's gracious invitation and not to allow their hearts to become hard—like the hearts of the children of Israel in the wilderness. And then he describes the actions of those days. The Israelites, for their part, rebelled and put God on trial, in spite of

---

[10] I am not saying that the event in history is the cause of God's knowledge of it in eternity. I am not comfortable with the idea that knowledge is caused by the things known. God's knowledge is intuitive. I will deal with foreknowledge in subsequent chapters.

having observed his works (vv. 8–9). In response, God was grieved for forty years and said the people were straying in their hearts and ignorant of him (v. 10). Consequently, in his wrath he swore, "They will not enter my rest" (v. 11).

That all this was real interaction between God and Israel, taking place in the Sinai wilderness soon after Israel's flight from Egypt, is clear. That the passage is time bound is seen in the fact that God's grieving lasted forty years specifically, for example—not forever. That the language is anthropathic—see chapters 1 and 2—is beside the point; God by his own affirmation is relating to time. Furthermore, God's decisive oath of judgment came then and there and in response to Israel's spiritual infidelity.

That is what transpired in the real world. Israel turned aside from trusting obedience, and God became angry and made a decision that condemned all the adult generation (except for Joshua and Caleb) to die in the wilderness during forty years of nomadic wandering. That is the way the Bible presents the history, and that is the way it should be read.

Whatever God knew and decided in eternity must be understood in light of the real history when Israel tested God repeatedly and angered him and he concluded judgment. Both Israel and God were acting—interacting—in the world of time and space that we inhabit. Once again, influence and response were at work.

There is no shortage of passages that look back into history to see the acts of God there. Psalm 99 notes that Moses, Aaron, and Samuel were among those who called upon Yahweh, and "he answered them" (v. 6). Indeed, "He spoke to them in a pillar of cloud," which was very much an object in the world of time and space (v. 7). This was real interaction between God and human beings, and it took place in real time and space. No other explanation of the events is appropriate for understanding them, including anything God did or decided in his eternal state of being. The passage anchors the events in this world and makes no reference to God's acts, knowledge, or decisions in eternity. Much less does the passage explain the this-worldly actions of God or humans in terms of eternal decisions or knowledge.

Such awareness of the past serves to ground anticipated interaction with God in the present. Thus the psalmist counts on Yahweh to hear and answer:

"Listen closely to me; / answer me quickly when I call" (102:2). This reckoning, that God will hear and act in response, is in every way time bound. Nothing in eternity is called on to provide context or meaning for the expectation.

The speech of Stephen in Acts 7 moves along the very same lines and does not need detailed attention. It makes many references to what God did in the history of his dealings with Israel, among them the following. He spoke to Abraham in a number of different times and places (vv. 3, 6, 7). He talked with Moses from the burning bush (vv. 31–32). He both saw the affliction of the Israelites and heard their outcry and as a result came down to deliver them (v. 34). Especially crucial, in response to their idolatry, then he "turned away and gave them up to worship the stars of heaven" (v. 42). None of this is said to have taken place in the eternal plan of God, although he saw it all and provided for it all there. All of it took place in the real world as described in the biblical record, and all of it took place in terms of the free human and divine interactions that record states or implies.

Perhaps I should expect readers to agree with what I am saying and to ask why I am stating the obvious. The answer is that far too many theologians look at all such passages through the lens of theological speculation about who God is forever. Determinists are particularly guilty of this; they find the ultimate meaning of these recollections and prayers in God's eternal knowledge and decrees. This has the effect of mitigating the significance of the interaction in time and space, in real history, and of interpreting that history as eternally predetermined. Our perspective instead ought to be on the interaction in history. That is where God acts, and that is where we grasp the real meaning of the biblical record. Whatever things mean in eternity, they mean the same as in time and space, the arena in which God has chosen to act and which the Bible describes as the real history.

5. Acts 12 and the Role of Angels

Regarding angels, Heb 1:14 asks a rhetorical question expecting the answer yes: "Are they not all ministering spirits sent out to serve those who are going to inherit salvation?" This establishes a couple of things: (1) that angels—whether "guardian angels" or not—act in this world on behalf of the people of God; and (2) that they are sent forth by God for this purpose. Such angelic acts, therefore, are indirectly but certainly the acts of God in time and space.

Any number of passages could be used to illustrate this. Acts 12:3–19 provides a helpful and interesting example. Basking in the warm reception given his execution of James, son of Zebedee, Herod Agrippa I—"king" of Judea, AD 41–44—decided to arrest Peter, apparently planning his death too. In prison in Jerusalem, Peter was guarded closely, around the clock, by four squads of guards—each a group of four, two to whom he was chained and two on watch outside the cell door.[11] The church was praying for him.

Suddenly, an angel appeared in the cell. Peter was sleeping soundly, but the angel's sharp touch awakened him; the chains fell from his wrists. Apparently in shock, Peter had to be told what to do: "Get dressed . . . put on your sandals. . . . Wrap your cloak around you . . . follow me" (v. 8). Indeed Peter thought it was all a dream. Soon they were past the guard posts and came to the main gate, which opened automatically, and they were outside. The angel departed, and Peter became fully aware of what had happened and went to the house of his relatives, Mary and her son John Mark.

Soon he was explaining to those gathered there to pray. He understood and confessed that "the Lord had brought him out of the prison" (v. 17). The angel's work was, indeed, the Lord's work—regardless of whether "Lord" here means God the Father or the Lord Jesus specifically.

God had once again intervened in human history, in the world of time and space and chains and clothes and soldiers and prison cells. He had done so with a keen sense of timing, on the very eve when Peter would have been brought out for judgment the following day. And everything the Bible describes happened then and there, not in eternity.

To be sure, God planned for this in eternity, but he acted to work miracles in a prison in Jerusalem not long before Agrippa's untimely

---

[11] See F. F. Bruce, *Commentary on the Book of Acts, NICNT*, rev. ed. (Grand Rapids: Eerdmans, 1988), 248.

death in AD 44. And that action was prompted by Peter's imprisonment and impending martyrdom, which was in turn brought about by Herod Agrippa's wicked decision to please the Jewish establishment by eliminating those who promoted the Way, as the practice of early Christianity is sometimes called in Acts. When making his plans in eternity, God foresaw all of this and incorporated it all in his plan.

This was not some standard operating procedure for God. Yes, he delivered Peter, but he permitted Agrippa to execute James. He alone knows the reasons for the difference, but they illustrate well the different ways things develop in the world where God is at work—the contingencies, in other words.

For that matter, the same chapter recounts the act of yet another angel sent by God. Agrippa had gone back to the royal residence at Caesarea after the incident involving Peter and was roundly glorified by emissaries from Tyre and Sidon. They spoke of him as a god, and he did not reject their adoration. Immediately, an angel struck him, "because he did not give the glory to God" (v. 23). He died soon thereafter.

Once more, this was an act of God in the world of time and space, prompted then and there by Agrippa's ungodly abrogation to himself of God's glory—and perhaps by his wicked execution of James and attempt on Peter. Both of these angels, representing the hand of the Lord who directed them, acted in human history in the mode of influence and response. The acts reflected decisions made—even if in eternity—in the context of what was happening in the world of time and space.

Many similar examples are available. Consider the visit of the three "angels"—one of them Yahweh himself—to Abraham and Sarah, described in Genesis 18. The account contains a number of highly unusual representations. These include: (1) the Lord's questioning within himself as to what to tell Abraham (v. 17); (2) the Lord's saying he will "go down" to Sodom to see whether what he has heard is so, and "If not, I will find out" (v. 21); and (3) the famous "bargaining" between Abraham and the Lord over how many righteous must be there for him to spare the city (vv. 23–32). Chapter 19 continues the story with the well-known activity of the two angels visiting Lot's house and acting in the situation.

To be sure, Bible interpreters will insist that these anthropomorphic wordings are not to be taken literally. Surely the Lord did not ask himself whether and how much to tell Abraham. Surely the Lord didn't have to "go down" to Sodom to learn anything at all. Surely he did not really bargain with Abraham about the number of righteous persons in Sodom. Yes, the wording is dramatized to enable us to get the main points. All the same, there is univocal meaning in them. God is intervening in human history. He is acting in time and space, in the real-life situations of Abraham and Sarah and Lot and his family and Sodom and Gomorrah. That is where the real interaction, the influence and response, takes place, not in eternity. We should define God's plan in eternity to match what the record describes in temporal history.

6. Ephesians 2 and Other Passages Describing the Human Experience of Redemption

Especially helpful are biblical passages describing the experience of redemption. Any number of them will provide examples. Only a few must suffice, starting with Ephesians 2. The chapter presents strong contrast between the conditions of people before and after they are converted. This contrast appears in vv. 1–10 in a way that speaks especially of the individual, and in vv. 11–22 especially of the people of God corporately. These are veritable "before and after" pictures.

In the experience of individuals, vv. 1–3 describe the before picture and vv. 4–10 the one afterward. The readers were spiritually dead and objects of God's wrath. After their conversion they are spiritually alive and recipients of God's grace. This is a narrative of events taking place in time and space, not of transactions in eternity. The death and wrath were real, and so is the change to life and grace.

The account in the latter half of the chapter is equally dramatic. As a people, the Gentile readers addressed were without God and hope, aliens, not a part of the covenant people of God (v. 12). Now, instead, they are fellow citizens with the saints and members of God's family (v. 19).

All of this is time bound. There is a before and an after. Before conversion they were outsiders. When they came to faith their situation changed, and they became citizens of the kingdom of God. Only when they heard the gospel and believed did they move, in transformation, from one set of circumstances to the other.

First Thessalonians 1:9, with pointed brevity, characterizes the readers' experience as having "turned to God from idols to serve the living and true God." First Corinthians 6:9–11 first presents a sharp contrast between those who practice various sins and the Christian readers. Then Paul says dramatically: "Some of you used to be like this." What they were previously they are no longer. They have moved from the past to the present. Titus 3:3–6 speaks of this in a way that includes Paul himself: "We too were once foolish, disobedient, deceived, enslaved by various passions and pleasures, living in malice and envy, hateful, detesting one another. But when the kindness of God our Savior and his love for mankind appeared, he saved us . . . through the washing of regeneration and renewal by the Holy Spirit."

Whether in these passages or in scores of others one could cite, the record speaks clearly of human experiences during their lives on planet Earth. People who were lost have been found. Those spiritually dead have been made alive. The condemned have been justified. Previously under the power of darkness, they have been translated into the kingdom of God's dear Son (Col 1:13). "You were once darkness, but now you are light in the Lord" (Eph 5:8).

These passages, like much of the Bible's narrative, are not describing events that took place in eternity. They who have been transformed by God's redemptive work in Christ and by the Holy Spirit are not being viewed as the "elect" before their salvation in time. The "elect" are the people of God. These were previously not the people of God; they were lost and unregenerate sinners, aliens, dead and in darkness: "While [they] were still sinners, Christ died for [them]" (Rom 5:8). They remained sinners until, also in space and time, they were personally regenerated, and only then did they become the saints of God. Before the new birth, and without it, they were bound for hell. And their situation in life and before God did not change, not even when Jesus died on the cross, until they were saved by grace through faith. (If, in fact, the work of Christ had already saved them—in AD 30 or 33?—they were never lost.)

To be sure, God had an eternal plan that he settled on before time began. I would not deny that or the eternal election of believers (1 Cor 1:21), but election in eternity does not make men "elect" in time while they are still his enemies. The Bible, in passages like those cited here, is describing events in the real, temporal, biblical world of our existence and history. Jesus's redemptive work is not effective until it is applied,[12] and it is not applied in eternity. Once again, we should read the Bible as it presents itself to us, as an account of God and humankind in space and time.[13] In some way, then, we begin to realize that there is a coinciding, some kind of identity between eternity and time. The unknown God of eternity is the God of time. I will return to this matter in a subsequent chapter.

---

[12] For an excellent discussion of this by a long-respected Calvinist, see the masterful "Vicarious Atonement" in Shedd, *Dogmatic Theology*, 2:378–488, esp. 438–41, 474–80 (see chap. 2, n. 6).

[13] I assume it obvious that I would reject any attempt to define the events in time and space as merely phenomenological, thus making it necessary to find their real meaning in the will of God. Nothing in Scripture sets up such a dichotomy between God's eternal will and events in history.

SIX

Reading the Bible: Examples of God at Work in This World (Part II)

More examples from Scripture depict God at work in this world of time and space and help us read the Bible correctly. In the previous chapter, I chose examples that speak more broadly. In this chapter are examples that are typically narrower in scope, focusing especially on specific incidents that involve human contingency and divine foreknowledge—which will become the subject of some chapters to follow.

1. Genesis 22 and What God Learned from Abraham's Obedience

Several biblical passages represent God as knowing what has been "learned" from human activity. Genesis 22:1–14, when God directed Abraham to sacrifice Isaac, offers a good example. Abraham obeyed—immediately, as far as we can tell from the narrative. To be sure, he believed that in some way God would provide for Isaac to be the covenant heir anyway, as indicated by his words to the accompanying servants: "*We'll* come back to you" (v. 5), emphasis added. And Heb 11:19 reads the record to mean that he accounted that God was able to raise Isaac from the dead—an astounding exercise of faith!

In Abraham's heart, then, he did to his son what he might have done to any sacrificial animal. Had God not stopped him, the act would have been finished. But God stopped him and said something that compels our attention: "Now I know that you fear God" (v. 12). Ah! Does that mean that God "learned," then and there, from Abraham's obedience?

Some biblical interpreters, like the open theists, say that he did and that this means he did not know it before. Thus they deny not merely God's foreknowledge but his immutability. Others suggest that God already knew what Abraham would do and that his knowledge of it settled that Abraham would obey. Taken this way, the wording—"Now I know"—is mere "accommodation," told that way so that we can understand the episode. Furthermore, taken this way, the event itself must be reinterpreted as something God had programmed in advance.

Neither of these approaches leads aright. The world of Abraham and Isaac in whatever year BC that was, with the wood and the knife and the ram caught in the thicket, and God interacting with them then and there, was and is the real world. The Bible presents it that way, and that is the way we ought to read it. What happened between God and Abraham happened only there and really involved their mutual influence and response. And when the Lord said, "Now I know," he was speaking truthfully: simply, "Now that you have obeyed, I know that you fear me."

Did God know this already? Certainly, but he knew it from Abraham's obedience and only from—that is, (logically) "following"—that obedience. "Now—in consequence of your obedience—I know that you fear God"; that is the exact truth about what transpired, and it is the truth that matters. Sure, God knew it from before the foundation of the world, but he knew it even then (if there is a "then" in eternity) only in consequence of Abraham's obedience of God in time. (More about this relationship in subsequent chapters.)

There is no reason to think, by the way, that God knew this about Abraham because he put Abraham in a set of circumstances where the only choice he had was to obey. Nothing in the biblical account suggests such a thing. We live in the here and now, and God really interacts with us here and now. The full meaning of this interaction is here and now. The decisions that determine things are made here and now. God's knowledge and purposes in eternity were to test Abraham and respond appropriately, whether he obeyed or disobeyed.

2. 1 Samuel 23, Foreknowledge, and David at Keilah

The Bible gives numerous examples of divine-human interaction when God's foreknowledge and human contingencies are involved. The situation of David at Keilah in 1 Sam 23:9–13 is an excellent example.

David was attempting to stay away from the reaches of Saul and—presumably by means of the Urim and Thummim—asked God if Saul would come to Keilah for him. The answer was unequivocal: "The Lord answered, 'He will come down.'" Then David asked whether in that eventuality the people of Keilah would betray him to Saul. Again, the answer was definite: "They will."

In fact, neither of these things happened, even though God said they would. Was he wrong? No, contingency was involved—and contingency does not have to be stated to be present.[1] When subsequent events reveal that contingency was present, we recognize the contingency. God understands contingencies and foreknows events accordingly. He knew what would transpire if David stayed there, and by revealing that information he provided the impetus for David to move out of the danger. This

---

[1] Some philosophically inclined theologians say that God knows counterfactuals; that is, he knows what will happen in situations contrary to fact, in situations that never develop. He is omniscient, he knows "all possible worlds." And nothing about that knowledge lessens the reality of events in the real world. The situation of David at Keilah is a good example. I will deal with the issue of counterfactuals in a subsequent chapter.

is a wonderful example both of what God knows and how he uses his knowledge to influence the response of human beings without coercing their wills.

We need to view what happened in the very way the narrative presents it. In the real world, David could relocate or remain in Keilah and be captured by Saul. God knew what would happen if he stayed and revealed that to David. David decided to go elsewhere when he could have decided to stay. The future that certainly would have been obtained in one contingent "world" (set of circumstances) was replaced by the future that certainly awaited in another such "world." God foreknew both worlds. Perhaps it would be better to say he "knew" both worlds, since I prefer to limit foreknowledge to the world that actually obtains[2]—and influenced David from one to the other, in real time and space.[3]

The relationship between divine foreknowledge, or prescience, and human freedom can be confusing. Most people, theologians or not, find it convincing that, if God knows that a given event will take place, that event must (of necessity) take place. This is not true, and I will attempt to show this in a subsequent chapter. It is enough to say, here, that the knowledge of events, even foreknowledge of them, is grounded in the events themselves, not vice versa. Foreknowledge does not fix the future. Whatever the case, in eternity God determined to deal with David in the very way he did—that is, in the way that allowed David to choose freely between staying and going.

3. Jonah 3 and the Lord's Change of Plans

Passages that represent the Lord as changing plans are especially helpful in this discussion. One example of this claimed our attention in chapter 2, in

---

[2] Foreknowledge will be the subject of more than one chapter to follow.

[3] I am not fond of "possible worlds" terminology; at best, it is useful only as a means of discussing logical possibilities. It may well be that this world is the only one that is actually possible. I will return to this subsequently.

discussing whether God repents or changes his mind. Another example that fits well the discussion in this section appears in Jonah 3:10.

The narrative that lies behind this is well known. After Jonah's experience in the belly of the great sea creature, God spoke to him a second time and directed him to go preach to the Ninevites what he would tell him. Jonah obeyed—without further hesitation, it appears—and began proclaiming what God told him to say: "In forty days Nineveh will be demolished!" (v. 4). To Jonah's surprise—and dismay, it seems—they repented, led by their king (vv. 5–9). Jesus would later confirm that the repentance was genuine (Luke 11:32). In consequence, the text relates, "God saw their actions—that they had turned from their evil ways—so God relented from the disaster he had threatened them with. And he did not do it" (Jonah 3:10).

Here are foreknowledge and contingency again, as well as the foreplanning of God. What we have to do is rule out possibilities at either extreme. At one end, this does not mean that the Ninevites' repentance surprised God and he changed his eternal plan on the spot. At the other end, neither does it mean that in eternity, before the world existed, God settled this in such a way that it was all predetermined and the human participants could not have chosen differently. In the latter scenario, Jonah and the people of Nineveh were playing out, in time and space, a drama that had already played out, before they existed, in the mind of God.

The way we ought to view this is the way it is presented in the biblical narrative. Given their wickedness, God had determined to destroy them and gave them forty days' notice. The contingency involved, though unstated, was real; they could repent or not. They did, and God decided to spare them instead.

Reading the passage this way, as consisting of the momentous decisions of God and human beings in time and space, acting in influence and response mode, by no means contradicts the idea that God was working his eternal plan. All one has to do to see this is to recognize that God's eternal plan includes real contingencies in time. His actions in such contingent situations ultimately accomplish his plan. God and men were influencing and responding to each other, then and there. That is where we discern the meaning of the events, where both God and men were making decisions and interacting. We ought not move the decisions back into eternity.[4]

Did God know and plan for all this in advance? Of course! Even so, the drama that played out in real time and space was the real interaction. The plan in eternity included everything that transpired in time: the decision to destroy, the announcement, the repentance, and a new decision. But these things really transpired in time and space. God responded to the Ninevites' free decision, in time, to repent.[5] Even when planning in eternity, logically prior to time, he responded to the decision they made in time[6]— and was still perfectly successful in bringing about the accomplishment of his purpose.

Everything in the plan depended on everything in real time, in other words. What God "did" in the plan meant, in ultimate reality, the same as what he did in dealing with Nineveh and Jonah. Everything that transpired in actual history had exactly the same meaning it would have had if God himself had come into existence when he created the world and had no foreknowledge at all. (Which, of course, is utterly impossible.)

We must not let our comprehension of God in eternity swallow up God in time. Someone will say, neither must we let God in time swallow up God in eternity, which is equally true. But God in time is the God we know for sure, the God revealed in the Scriptures. God in eternity, for us, is the God we reason our way to by means of his self-revelation. And in doing that we had better remember Deut 29:29: "The hidden things belong to the LORD

---

[4] Again, I am not denying that God made decisions in eternity, but we should not think of his eternal decision as being prior to, so as to be determinative of, his acts in time. In a subsequent chapter, I will discuss the possibility of some coincidence between eternity and time.

[5] As this work will make clear, by "free" decision I mean to affirm libertarian freedom, that the Ninevites actually could have made a different choice.

[6] I call attention to the tenses I use in such statements, not saying he determined to do something or knew something because the persons involved would do such and such, but because they did such and such. Regardless how that sounds, that is the proper relationship between God's knowledge and decisions in eternity and events in time. God knows in eternity what we did in time.

our God, but the revealed things belong to us and our children forever." Perhaps we need to begin thinking of God in eternity as the same as God in time and then allow the latter to form our theology.

We simply do not understand fully how to put God's actions in a space-time world into our concept of eternity. In some way beyond our comprehension, the two realms must coincide or intersect. For our metaphysics, we need to understand that there is a sense in which God's actions in time and space and his "decisions" in eternity have exactly the same ultimate meaning. We separate them in peril for our understanding of him. Our surest understanding is of how he has revealed himself in the Bible, in the context of the world he made.

In sum, there is no contradiction between what God knows and plans in eternity and what transpires in the real world of time and space. Everyone will agree with that, but some will let their a priori concept of eternal meaning color their understanding of the real-world meaning. That is the wrong way to view things. God's creation, in his eternity, of a space-time, constantly changing world makes this the real arena of his interactions with the characters in the biblical narrative and with us. So we must understand who he is in eternity by who he is in time and space. And when events in history manifest contingency and freedom of choice for human beings, God's knowledge and purposes in eternity will not contradict that. He knows and has planned for history the way it is described in Scripture.

4. Isaiah 38, Contingency, and Hezekiah's Prayer

The biblical record often presents contingencies in divine-human encounters, situations that present themselves as capable of happening one way or another. Any number of examples are available to us. The interaction between God and Hezekiah in Isaiah 38 (cf. 2 Kgs 20:1–11) instructs us in this truth. With Isaiah as spokesman, God informed Hezekiah that he must set his house in order, that he would not live. Hezekiah immediately turned to God in prayer. Before Isaiah could even get away from the palace premises, God instructed him to return and inform Hezekiah that he had heard his prayer, seen his tears, and would heal him and add fifteen years to his life.

We are compelled to take every part of that at full face value. God had determined to end Hezekiah's life. When he said, "You are about to die; you will not recover" (v. 1), he meant right away, and Hezekiah understood that. The king would have died then had no contingency been involved. But Hezekiah prayed, and God heard and added fifteen years that Hezekiah would not have enjoyed had he not prayed. And all of this transpired then and there to the king of Judah on a definite date.

This is a valuable lesson for human-divine interaction in real time. God knew—perhaps from his own decision but in his omniscience regardless—and announced that Hezekiah was about to die. But there was contingency involved, even though the record does not say so, as the following events clearly demonstrate. Hezekiah chose, when he could have chosen some other response, to pray. Because of the prayer, God determined to add to his life. He would have died in about 700 BC, but he did not die until about 685 BC. There was real change in the real world, and God's actions were part of that. The record is clear, and our concept of God in eternity does not mean we should read something different into the account.

Again, discussions of this lead to discussions of foreknowledge. What did God know when he sent Isaiah the first time? I will discuss how foreknowledge is to be understood in subsequent chapters. For now, the obvious truth is that our reasoning about foreknowledge needs to have no impact at all on our understanding of what the biblical record presents us. Indeed, the record makes no reference to foreknowledge other than to what is implied in God's statement that Hezekiah was about to die.

If we are unable to fit foreknowledge into our understanding of the record, that inability is more likely to lie in our understanding of how God's foreknowledge works for him than in our understanding of what the Bible describes.[7] And what the Bible describes is clear and easily understood: God

---

[7] Kevin Hester suggested, when reading this paragraph, that in the Bible, God speaks to us "anthropocentrically," that it is "a revelation from God to humans and

signaled the end of Hezekiah's life, Hezekiah prayed, and God gave him an additional fifteen years. That's exactly what the record communicates, and that's what was real. The interaction was not in some eternal realm other than the time-and-space realm in Judah about a century before the Babylonian captivity. Once we learn to read eternity in light of the revelation of God in history, we rest content in understanding that God knew and purposed forever to do exactly what the Bible says he did: confront Hezekiah, allow him the freedom to respond, and then respond accordingly.

This is also a good example of the effectiveness of prayer, by the way. Prayer changes things in the real world, even if to say this sounds trite. As a result of prayer, God does things he would not do apart from prayer—and he incorporates all those things into his unfailing plan.

It is possible to view this as an instance of God's having predetermined that Hezekiah would pray, which would make the interaction something other than what the record presents it to be. I see no signal in the text that we should read it in such a way.

5. Jeremiah 18, God's Repentance, and Live Options for Human Beings

An example that speaks of God repenting in a context of live options appears in the familiar account of Jeremiah's visit to a potter's house, in Jer 18:1–12. A careful analysis of the passage provides insight into God's interaction with human beings in the world of time and space.

The Lord sends Jeremiah to observe a potter at work (vv. 1–3). The potter sees that a vessel in the making is flawed, so he reshapes the clay into the very vessel he wanted it to be (v. 4).

At this point the Lord gives Jeremiah the lesson to draw from what he has observed (vv. 5–10), and it is in three parts: (1) The clay being shaped

---

for humans," revealing "what we need to know . . . in a way we can understand." Thus all of Scripture speaks truly, but we need not expect it to describe God fully except as it communicates his desired relationship with us.

by the potter corresponds to the people of Israel whom God is shaping (v. 6). Following this, the Lord gives two possibilities for Judah—or for any people. (2) One possibility: Though the Lord speaks to judge a people for wickedness, if they genuinely repent he will "relent," or, repent of—turn from—the judgment he has intended to administer (vv. 7–8). (3) The alternative possibility: Though the Lord speaks to bless a people with good, if they turn away from him in disobedience he will "relent"—turn from—the blessing he has intended to bring (vv. 9–10).

Then the Lord instructs Jeremiah what to say, in God's name, to Judah: that the first of those two possibilities is already in play (vv. 11–12). The Lord has pronounced judgment; indeed, he has fashioned and devised it. Consequently, they must repent and turn from their evil ways (v. 11)—ways defined more clearly in v. 15. The clear implication, of course, is that if they do so the Lord will turn from the judgment and bring blessing instead. However—as is true throughout Jeremiah's prophecy—it is clear that Judah will not repent. They are determined to continue in the wicked imaginations of their hearts (v. 12).

The theological implications are clear enough, although there is both a similarity and a dissimilarity between the potter with the clay and the Lord with the people of Judah (or any other nation). The similarity is that the people, like the clay for the potter, are the Lord's work. He makes them into what he pleases or wills to make them. God's sovereignty is at work in this.

The dissimilarity is that vessels of clay have no wills of their own, while people do. And so the Lord affirms that his judgment or blessing will depend on whether the people decide for or against him. Both possibilities are live options, and either God's judgment or his blessing can be canceled depending on the choice of the people.

In other words, to cite God's sovereignty in the matter—that is, his unconditional right to make vessels of his choosing—does not in and of itself say what vessels he chooses to make or why. It is his sovereign right to make vessels according to any condition he wishes to establish, and he establishes his condition clearly. If people repent of their wickedness, the sovereign God pleases to bless them. And vice versa.

The passage speaks in the context of time and space. God presents himself as having pronounced a curse or a blessing. Then he establishes that the people may choose an option he has given them. Indeed, in the case of Judah, he appeals to them to choose repentance, and he promises that he will respond accordingly. He has sovereignly determined that their response, in time and space, will make the difference in determining which future they will obtain.

Is there anything in the passage to indicate that Judah is, because of her depravity, totally disabled, unable to respond to the Lord's gracious invitation? Perhaps, and perhaps not. We may look for the answer in one short clause in v. 12, indicating that they said, "It's hopeless." If they mean, "We can't help ourselves," then perhaps that is an admission that they cannot find it within themselves to turn from their evil ways. Indeed, all sinners are unable to turn to God without his initiating, enabling grace, but they are not likely to acknowledge that inability.

The exact meaning of this little affirmation needs close examination, then; it is a matter of some dispute, not necessarily tied to theological concerns. The ESV renders, "That is in vain!" The NIV has, "It's no use." Linked as it is with the rest of the affirmation in v. 12, it is far more likely that Judah is saying something like, "There's no hope for what you're asking, because we're determined to go our own way. It's vain and useless for you to ask this." The entire response is of one piece, in which "the people reject [this call] disdainfully, replying that they are resolved to abide by their evil courses."[8] They are stubbornly ridiculing the effort to turn them away from their evil ways.

Manifestly, no wicked person can turn away from sin, to God, apart from strong and gracious help by God. This involves the proclamation of his word and the enlightening, convicting, enabling work of the Holy Spirit of God, using that word. Even so, the circumstance of unreachability does arise in the hearts of some who have hardened themselves beyond any hope. Then,

---

[8] Carl Friederich Keil and Franz Delitzsch, "Jeremiah," in *Old Testament Commentaries*, vol. 5 (Grand Rapids: Associated Publishers and Authors, 2000), 732.

even if it was too late for Judah to repent, we should remember that vv. 7–10 provide a more general statement about how the Lord works in principle.

A question arises as to whether this passage in Jeremiah, in particular, was in Paul's mind when he wrote Rom 9:21–23. It is possible that Paul was thinking of it, at least in a general way. But specific things are in Romans that are not in Jeremiah: that a potter, and God, are at liberty to make vessels for honor (mercy) and vessels for dishonor (wrath). There is nothing in Jeremiah that corresponds to this; the vessel that was "marred" on the wheel was, in fact, remade into a good vessel. And the two possibilities in Jeremiah are not mentioned in Romans—a fact that is often conveniently overlooked by those who discuss Romans 9. Again, Paul's appeal to God's sovereign right, as valid as it is in saying that God shows mercy to whomever he wills, does not answer the question, To whom does he desire to show mercy? The rest of Romans 9 and 10 goes on to answer that question: God desires to show mercy to those who seek the righteousness that comes by faith (9:30–33; 10:3–12).

Clearly, then, the lesson in Jeremiah 18, drawn from the prophet's visit to the potter's house, concerns what happens in time and space, not what happened before the foundation of the world. Like the potter with his lump of clay, Yahweh was at work to mold Judah into the vessel he desired. But the final outcome would turn on the condition he had established. He had already pronounced judgment, but if they would repent he would turn from that judgment to blessing—just as the potter remade the lump of clay into the vessel he desired.

All this did not happen in eternity, nor does the passage appeal to any decision of God in eternity. Instead, God and Judah were interacting in the real world of Jeremiah's day to implement a principle of God's dealings that applies at any time and place. The choices that God and human beings make in time involve influence and response and form the conditions for the interaction. We should understand that in eternity God knew and purposed to interact with human beings in that way.

The Knowledge of Eternal God about Time and Space

SEVEN

The Problem of Foreknowledge— and the Solution

Everything so far is an aspect of the relationship between eternity and time, between God as he is in himself eternally and God as he creates, sustains, and acts within the realm of the space-time cosmos we are part of. The creation of this cosmos is of momentous significance, an apparent— but only apparent—contradiction of God's immutability. God has chosen to make a world and put us in it and then to make that world the arena in which he acts and interacts with us. Among other things, this means we ought to understand God's eternal purposes by understanding, first, what he has done in time and revealed in Scripture.

I move now to apply this same principle to the way we understand God's knowledge, which we call foreknowledge when we conceive of God as knowing, in eternity, what will transpire in time and space before it occurs there. Some of the examples in the previous two chapters directly involve foreknowledge. If we can fathom the relationship between God's exhaustive foreknowledge and the reality of events in history, we can probably understand other issues involved in the relationship between God's eternal purposes and his acts in time. Understanding God's foreknowledge, in respect to the reality of the space-time world and all that occurs here, is a matter for several chapters.

The Relationship between Eternal Foreknowledge and Events in Time

First, however, understanding foreknowledge requires a word about God's eternal knowledge and the course of time in our world. On the one hand, God's knowledge is eternal. He has known forever everything he knows; he never learns anything new. Considered only in relation to himself, there is no "fore" knowledge for God since there is no before and after, no succession of events in God's eternal, immutable, omniscient existence.

On the other hand, although he knows all the events of time eternally, he knows them for what they are: events in time. To say this differently, he knows everything eternally, not temporally. He does not gain knowledge of a 2020 event after he gained knowledge of a 1920 event. Even so, he knows temporal events as temporal events. Thus, he knows the difference between one day and another, as the creation week demonstrates. He knows that the assassination of John F. Kennedy is in the past and that the end of the COVID-19 pandemic is (as I write this) yet in the future—if indeed the pandemic will end. But these are past and future from the perspective of beings in the world of time and space, and they are really past and future in this world that God created to operate with a past and future. He knows this world perfectly.

Consequently, when we speak of "fore"knowledge, we mean that God knew yesterday, and every day since the time of Gen 1:1, what everyone is doing today and will do every day until Jesus comes—and beyond that. But yesterday, today, and the future are real in our world and from our perspective.

It is proper, then, to speak of "fore"knowledge, since we are speaking correctly out of our temporal existence. As Helm observes, for God to know the "future" is to know it as future to those in time.[1] In our world, it is always true that God knows what will transpire before it transpires.

This is the perspective from which we speak and from which we must speak. When we speak this way we speak truth in the real world. God himself may not have any succession of events within himself, or experience any duration of time,[2] but he knows perfectly well what succession of events is really occurring in our world and can act with us within the framework of those events. That he created this world justifies this implication. So does the fact that he is sustaining or upholding the world and all its events. So does the fact that God the Son entered this world in time and space.

The Logical Problem

Without question, divine foreknowledge appears to present a problem, at least a logical one, for human freedom and contingencies in the real world—and so far the way I have suggested that the biblical narrative should be read. To state this problem is relatively simple: if God knows in advance what will transpire in the real world, then what he knows must therefore transpire. This conclusion seems indisputably logical to most people, theologians or otherwise.

Expressing this in specific and personal terms makes it a little easier to discuss. If God knows I am going to do any particular thing in the future, regardless how significant or insignificant, apparently I must, of necessity, do it. If I were to do something different from what God knows I will do, that would mean that God was mistaken, which is absurd and impossible on its face.

For traditional determinists, this claim seems to be conclusive against what we call "libertarian" human freedom in the real world, although there

---

[1] Helm, *Eternal God*, 100 (see chap. 1, n. 5). Also: "The concept of foreknowledge applies not to a timeless knower's knowledge of certain events or actions, but to a temporal agent's recognition of timeless knowledge under certain temporal circumstances" (98).

[2] I realize that some of this is debated by some theologians.

is more involved in their denial. As perhaps all will agree, God can foreknow only what is certain to be. For determinists, then, God has in eternity made all the events of human and cosmic history certain by his foreordination of those events. As Shedd puts this, God "could not have foreknown that [the crucifixion] would take place, unless he had predetermined that it should."[3] If that is correct, God's foreknowledge of the future rests on his foreordination of it. Furthermore, this means that all our actions must necessarily be what they are.

Libertarian freedom, by contrast, means that a person, at least at some choosing times, really can choose in more than one way. This ability is sometimes called the power of alternate choice and so represents a contingency. In other words, if people have libertarian freedom, there are occasions when they really could make choices different from the ones they actually make.

Determinists deny that such freedom actually exists in the world. Many of them use the word *freedom* to describe some human choices, but by this they mean that the person "freely" or voluntarily makes the only choice possible for him or her to make—a view called compatibilism or soft determinism.[4] Determinists therefore will agree that if God knows I am going to make a given choice, I must make it. But their reason for saying this goes beyond mere foreknowledge; it also involves God's foreordination or predetermining of all events, making all events "necessary." Those of us who believe that human beings have libertarian freedom do not think this "soft" deterministic concept of freedom is really freedom.

Determinists are not alone in saying that if God knows the future it must be as he knows it will be. Some neo-Arminian theologians, the open theists, have also accepted this logic. They agree that if God knows what a person is going to do tomorrow, when faced with a given choice, then the

---

[3] Shedd, *Dogmatic Theology*, 1:353 (see chap. 2, n. 6).

[4] Bruce A. Ware, *God's Greater Glory: The Exalted God of Scripture and the Christian Faith* (Wheaton: Crossway, 2004), 25, defines compatibilistic freedom thus: "When we choose and act, we do so from prevailing desires which explain exactly why *this* choice and not another is made. This obviously means, however, that when we choose, all things being just what they are, we *must* choose as we do."

person must make the choice he or she will make, the choice God already knows. Consequently, in order to protect human freedom, open theists deny that God has foreknowledge of such choices.[5] Some even suggest that if God knew, for example, that a given person was going to choose to sin, he would be responsible to stop the person from that course of action.

As the reader can see from this brief summary, determinists, when faced with God's sure foreknowledge of the future, wind up denying that humans are free to choose in any way other than the one way God knows, and has predetermined, that they will choose. Open theists, faced with the same logic—if God knows something, that something is necessary and cannot be otherwise—wind up denying God's foreknowledge.[6]

What this amounts to, whether by determinists or open theists or anyone else, brings us back to where this section began. On the surface, at least, there would appear to be a logical problem—a conflict or tension—between God's foreknowledge and human freedom. The two things do not seem to go together; they are not "compatible." Affirm foreknowledge and deny freedom, or affirm freedom and deny foreknowledge. Those are apparently the only two choices. If God knows what we are going to choose, we have to make that choice.

If God has exhaustive foreknowledge, the future is closed. Is that what we must acknowledge?

Solving the Problem

The answer to the preceding question is no. We do not have to choose between foreknowledge and libertarian freedom. We can affirm both. The solution lies in a careful analysis of all the "logic" involved. It turns out that

---

[5] Steven Lewis reminds me that process theology, as well as some other theologians like Richard Swinburne and Peter van Inwagen, hold views similar to those of open theists on this point.

[6] Kevin Hester thinks open theists accept the concept of foreknowledge as defined by determinists to include the element of foreordination. I will touch on the difference again in a subsequent chapter.

the logical problem is simply that: a logical problem, one we ourselves construct in the way we word things.

A careful consideration of all the logical factors involved will show that
foreknowledge does not contradict the freedom of human beings to choose
between alternatives. Especially with a phenomenon like eternal foreknowledge, in relation to a space-time world, logic can be a tricky thing, and some
of the elements, when analyzed more closely, help us avoid being forced into
viewing our cosmos as deterministic.

I have dealt with these logical issues elsewhere.[7] Here, then, I will focus
only, and relatively briefly, on the key factors involved. In doing so, I will
use a simple illustration throughout that can apply equally to all libertarian choices, whether consequential or trivial. This illustration assumes that
tomorrow I will be walking on a path through a park and will come to a
fork, where I may go either to the right or to the left, knowing that either
will bring me back where I began. God knows which way I am going to
choose. Will I be able to choose either of the two ways?

The answer is that I will be able to choose either way, even though God
knows the way I will choose. Here are some of the logical factors involved
in arguing for this answer.

First, knowledge of an event does not influence the event.[8] All that
is required to see the logic in this is to consider some past event we know
about. I know, for example, that Virginia defeated Texas Tech in the 2019
March Madness finals. Obviously, my knowing this fact had absolutely no
influence on the outcome, which was decided in the way basketball games
are decided, by the thousands of little contingencies—including many
human choices—that really could have been different. Obviously, had Texas
Tech won, my knowledge would be different from what it is.

[7] Robert E. Picirilli, "Foreknowledge, Freedom, and the Future," *JETS* 43
(2000): 259–71; "An Arminian Response to John Sanders's *The God Who Risks, A
Theology of Providence*," *JETS* 44 (2001): 467–91; *Grace, Faith, Free Will*, 50–63
(see preface, n. 4); *Free Will Revisited*, 79–88 (see chap. 5, n. 4).

[8] Davis, *Logic and the Nature of God*, 64 (see chap. 2, n. 4), says, "I cannot see
how knowledge, even divine foreknowledge, can be causally efficacious."

Just so with God's foreknowledge, which is, after all, knowledge about future facts. That he knows what I will choose before I choose it does not limit my choices. Knowledge of events is grounded in the events, not vice versa.[9] If I am going to choose the right fork tomorrow, he knows it in accord with the fact that I will do so. Likewise, if I am going to choose the left fork, he knows that. His knowledge of my choice depends on my choice and does not constrain it.[10]

God knew the outcome of the March Madness final game long before it occurred, but it was decided in exactly the way it was decided in the eyes of everyone who participated or observed without knowing the outcome in advance. In the same way, the announcement of Hezekiah's impending death, his prayer, and God's addition to his life were contingencies that, although God foreknew all the outcomes, were decided in time and space, exactly as the record presents them to us.

To be sure, as already noted, some theologians believe that God knows the future because he has already foreordained it. This deterministic move makes foreknowledge something more than knowledge. Suffice it to say, here, that those who say this are not really objecting to freedom on the

---

[9] Some theologians appear to regard knowledge of events as in some sense causal of the events. Steven Lewis mentioned Aquinas, *ST* 1.14.8: "The knowledge of God is the cause of things. For the knowledge of God is to all creatures what the knowledge of the artificer is to things made by his art." If this means that God's knowledge of an event, per se, is a cause of the event, I simply disagree. Furthermore, I do not think Aquinas meant that. He goes on to say, in the same place, "His knowledge must be the cause of things, *in so far as His will is joined to it.*" Again, in 1.14.9: "The knowledge of God, *joined to His will* is the cause of things. Hence it is not necessary that what ever God knows, is, or was, or will be; but only is this necessary as regards what He wills to be, or permits to be." (I have italicized the key words. See also 1.19.4 and 1.46.1, where God's will is the cause of things.) After writing this, I noted that Davis, *Logic and the Nature of God*, 64–65, makes the very same point.

[10] Davis, *Logic and the Nature of God*, 53 (whose book Matt Pinson pointed me to late in my preparation of this volume) expresses what I have just said: "What God knew yesterday is contingent upon what I will freely decide to do tomorrow." I think he successfully defends this claim.

grounds of foreknowledge, as such, but on the grounds of determinism. In effect, then, they argue from determinism to determinism. Certainly, if God has of his free will made all events necessary, human beings do not possess the freedom to choose between live options.

Second, and closely related, God's knowledge of a future event, including which fork I will choose tomorrow, logically implies only the certainty of that event, not its necessity.[11] This is an important distinction that one must master. Things that are certain include both contingencies (things that can be one way or another) and necessities (things that can be only the way they are). To describe an event as a necessity or contingency is to say something about its nature or cause. To describe an event as a certainty is only to say that it is or was or will be. All events are certainties.[12] The opposite of a certain future is not an uncertain future; it is no future at all.[13] To say that

---

[11] Scholastic theology, perhaps beginning with Aquinas, distinguished between two kinds of necessity: absolute and relative (or suppositional). See *ST* 1.19.3. (Steven Lewis also suggests Aquinas's *Summa Contra Gentiles*, 1.85.) Eric Phillips defines the difference in Thomas's categories thus: "Absolute necessity is necessity by definition. . . . Suppositional necessity . . . is based on a state of affairs. Socrates is able to sit or to stand, but 'granted that he is sitting, he must necessarily sit, as long as he is sitting.'" Phillips, quoting Aquinas, in "Absolute Necessity in Luther's de Servo Arbitrio," accessed May 31, 2020, www.pseudepigraph.us/2014/06/02 /absolute-necessity-in-luthers-de-servo-arbitrio/#sdfootnote15sym; no longer accessible. Perhaps my "certainty" corresponds to Aquinas's suppositional necessity. But my terminology is more easily understood and gets to the heart of the issues involved.

[12] My purpose here does not include arguing the origins of evil in the world. It is true that God actualized this world (out of all possibilities) with its certainties. But that is not what makes the certainties (when free choices are made) certainties. Free choices are not caused by outside forces; they arise from within the psyche and are self-determined. A choice is made certain by the making of the choice.

[13] Defining and using carefully these three terms—*certainty*, *necessity*, and *contingency*—is essential to any meaningful discussion of this issue. I do not insist that these are the only words that can possibly be used this way, or even that these words can only mean what I have defined them to mean. But I do insist that some set of words must be used to express these precise differences in meaning, else discussion becomes hopelessly confused. And anyone who gives either of these words a different meaning needs to find a word that fits the definition I have given, or else he or she risks misleading others when agreeing or disagreeing with me. In the sense

if God knows in advance that I will make a given decision then it is true that I will, is not (as Davis insightfully observes) a property of God's alone; if anyone knows correctly that I will make that choice, it is certain that I will make it.[14]

Alvin Plantinga provides an example of a careless use of terms that leads to faulty conclusions. He says, "It is logically necessary that if it was true eighty years ago that I will mow my lawn today, then I will mow my lawn today. It is therefore necessary that I will mow my lawn—necessary in just the sense in which the past is necessary. But then it is not within my power not to mow; hence I will mow freely."[15] This mixture of correct and incorrect calls for careful analysis. First, the opening sentence is correct, but one should note that "logically necessary" is not the same as an ontological necessity of the thing itself. Even here, then, "certain" would be better than "logically necessary." But in the second sentence, "necessary" is ambiguous. Does he now mean the necessity of the event itself and not merely the logical connection in the first sentence? If so, he is wrong; nothing more is justified from the first sentence (note "therefore") than the certainty that I will mow my lawn today. Ah, but then he makes a comparison: necessary in the same way the past is necessary. The ambiguity lies in whether he thinks (1) that all events of the past took place by a predetermined necessity, or (2) that once events happen they can no longer be undone and are "necessary" only in that logical sense. I think he means the second. If he means the first, then the final, concluding sentence is justified, but if he means the second, it is not. If the past is only "necessary" (read "certain") as what cannot be changed because it has already happened, Plantinga really can mow his lawn or not, and only if that is the case can he do so "freely." His mowing is what will make certain his mowing—even though God knows its certainty before he mows.

---

that I have used the three words, I understand determinists to believe that all events are necessities and that there are no real contingencies involved in human choices.

[14] Davis, *Logic and the Nature of God*, 54.

[15] Alvin Plantinga, "On Ockham's Way Out," *Faith and Philosophy* 3, no. 3 (July 1986): 238–39, cited in Helm, *Eternal God*, 128.

If I am going to choose the right fork tomorrow, God knows that event as certain. But—and this is very important—to say that it is certain is to say nothing more than that I will choose the right fork tomorrow. The "certainty" of an event is nothing more that its "eventness." It is true that if I am going to choose the right fork it is certain that I will. It is equally true that if I am going to choose the left fork it is certain that I will. Either can be the certainty, depending on which choice I will make.[16]

In neither case, however, is my choice a necessity. I have taken this walk many times, and each time I decide which fork I am going to take: sometimes the right, sometimes the left. There may be many factors influencing my choice at a given time, but influence does not eliminate my weighing whatever factors I choose to consider and then making a choice when I could very well choose the other. (I could even flip a coin.) This is a true contingency. Determinists simply believe that I can make only the choice I will make; thus their denial of libertarian freedom rests on the affirmation that alternative choices—true contingencies—are impossible and all choices are necessities.

There are such things as necessities, of course. The laws of nature bring us in contact with many. Sometimes God produces necessities that are outside the laws of nature, even in human conduct. Saul probably did not freely choose to prophesy all day, naked, before Samuel at Naioth (see 1 Sam 19:23–24). But to say that all events and choices are necessities goes far beyond logic, experience, and the biblical account of things.

David Hunt has argued in a way similar to this, using for an illustration the apparently random decay of a radioactive particle as registered by a Geiger counter. One can easily say after the fact, "This Geiger counter *emitted* a click at time *T*." Then before that happened it would be equally true that "This Geiger counter *will* emit a click at time *T*." To ask how the

---

[16] I see no need to involve the traditional philosophical-theological discussion of openness and closedness. That an event is certain is not the same thing as being closed. Contingencies are "open," and necessities are "closed." But this is to speak from our perspective, not from God's. And God knows that libertarian choices are "open" to us, even though he knows exactly which choice we will certainly obtain.

latter could be true before it occurred is "confused: that's just what it is for a statement to be about the *future!* . . . And because [it] was true, a being who failed to know [it] would not be omniscient."[17] Hunt concludes, "Because divine foreknowledge neither causes nor explains what it knows, it does not require us to adopt an attenuated understanding of free agency."[18]

Third, God's foreknowledge does not preclude his laboring sincerely with persons even when he knows they will choose against him. Why is this so? Because he knows that we really can choose against or for him—even if in some choices our depravity means that he must give grace (by his word and Spirit) to enable the choice for him. This follows immediately from the fact that such choices are contingencies and not necessities.

The choice I will make tomorrow, between the right and left paths, will not be made until I make the choice. In this world of time and space and human action, the future is open to human choices.[19] Today, the future is not fixed (unless by "fixed" one means, simply, "certain"; I use "fixed" as a synonym for "necessary"). And I will be the one to make the choice. I can make either, and God knows that I can. He knows contingencies as contingencies, and he knows the difference between them and necessities.

Why would God labor to persuade a person to do right even when he knows the person will do wrong? We do not always have access to God's reasons, but perhaps he does such a thing as the right thing to do. I say this because sometimes even we finite humans are faced with the need to say or do the right thing to someone in spite of the fact that the person has made clear that he or she is headstrong and will not heed our warning or appeal.

Whether we can explain why, the Bible makes clear that God labors with people even though he knows they will resist him. An excellent example of this appears in Jeremiah 36 in the matter of the scroll God directed

---

[17] David Hunt, "A Simple-Foreknowledge Response," in James K. Beilby and Paul R. Eddy, eds., *Divine Foreknowledge: Four Views* (Downers Grove, IL: IVP Academic, 2001), 49.

[18] Hunt, 102.

[19] It might not be accurate to say that the future is "open" to God, but it is correct to say that God knows the future as open to human choices.

Jeremiah to prepare. The whole book of Jeremiah reflects that God knew Judah would not turn back to him, but he spoke eloquently and movingly: "Perhaps when the house of Judah hears about all the disaster I am planning to bring on them, each one of them will turn from his evil way. Then I will forgive their iniquity and their sin" (Jer 36:3; cf. v. 7). Like the other examples in the previous two chapters, this passage needs to be read to mean just what it says: God was genuinely offering them a course they really could have pursued in spite of his knowing that they would not. And his eternal knowledge and purposes were to do just that.

Or perhaps God labors with those he knows will not repent in order to demonstrate his own character. Or there may be some reason we cannot fathom. But to say that he cannot labor sincerely with someone who will certainly reject him is simply to say more than we can possibly know—and more than the biblical teaching about God and his grace justifies. God knows how he "handles" his foreknowledge, of course, but we presume far too much to think we do. Perhaps the action of Jesus in John 18, though not entirely parallel, provides some understanding. Jesus, knowing everything that was to transpire, asked those who had come to arrest him, "Who is it that you're seeking?" (v. 4). He certainly knew the answer, but there was a reason to ask and prompt them.

It is likewise presumptuous to say that God cannot foreknow events that are true contingencies, events that human beings really can decide in more than one way. One can argue such an affirmation only on logical premises, making assumptions. However, our awareness and understanding of foreknowledge is not logically derived to begin with. We know about God's foreknowledge by way of his revelation of himself.[20] Then there is no convincing reason, logical or otherwise, to deny that God can know the outcome of truly free (libertarian) choices.[21] As William Lane Craig points

---

[20] Some may say that we also know of God's foreknowledge via natural theology. True or not, that is beside the point here.

[21] Keathley, *Salvation and Sovereignty*, 13 (see chap. 3, n. 18), observes, "How exactly God knows what free creatures will decide and choose remains unknown.

out, the burden of proof is on the objector: "Why should I know how God has such foreknowledge? Who are human beings that they should know how God foreknows the future?"[22] It seems self-evident that future facts are as "knowable" as past facts, and the omniscient God knows everything knowable. Whatever will be in the future is a certainty, and God knows it.

Of course, the way God works will depend on any number of factors. He may know, for example, that tomorrow, when I come to the fork in the path, there will be someone hiding along the right pathway to ambush a passerby. God has all sorts of means at his disposal, in his providence, to direct me to the other choice without constraining my will: a friend who encounters me there and wants to show me something on the other path, perhaps. God knows that I will be in danger if I choose the right fork and that I will be safe if I choose the left. He can see to it, one way or another, that I avoid the danger—if he wills. His knowledge of what I will do in certain circumstances does not force my choice. His use of such methods does not interfere with my freedom or even guarantee that I will make the choice he wants me to make.[23]

Not only does God know what will take place following either choice I make, he knows which choice I will make. Furthermore, that knowledge includes any intervention—any manipulation of circumstances—that he himself will bring to bear in the situation. We do not need to separate his plan for this in eternity from all the considerations that come into play in time and space. What he knows and decides in eternity incorporates everything in time and space in the very same way it would if he waited until the time and place

---

Some are bothered by this mystery"; he refers to this as the "grounding objection." He continues: "God knows all things and omniscience is an attribute of God. God innately knows our free choices by His very nature—by the very fact that He is God. Thus asking how God knows what genuinely free creatures will choose is the same as asking how it is that God is God."

[22] William Lane Craig, *The Only Wise God* (Grand Rapids: Baker, 1987), 118–21.

[23] In a later chapter, I will discuss God's knowledge of counterfactuals and his so-called middle knowledge.

to make the decisions. In David's situation at Keilah, cited earlier, God acted simply by revealing what David would encounter if he stayed in Keilah. Then David freely chose to leave—when he could have stayed.

Fourth, a real part of our supposed problem with foreknowledge is that we confuse ourselves logically with the illustrations we construct and the questions we pose. It seems very logical to say that if God knows I am going to choose the right fork, I cannot choose the left one. I note two things about this. First, well, sure. But we must think this through carefully: if I am going to choose one fork, I cannot choose the other. But that does not rob me of either option. Here, *cannot* is used logically, not to describe ability; and the reason is that the *if* clause already assumes the choice I will make. If I choose one way, it is that choice, not God's knowledge, that eliminates the other way.[24]

In order to clarify this "cannot" of logical impossibility, let me pose another illustration. Say I am given a coloring book and am directed to color a ball, on a certain page, with the color of my choice, from among the crayons available. I decide to color it blue. Having colored it blue, I cannot now go back and color it green or red or any other color. But it was the choice I made that eliminated the possibility of another choice, not God's (or anyone's) knowledge of that choice or even the certainty of the choice. My choice of blue is what made that choice certain.

Now bring foreknowledge into the illustration: God knew beforehand that I was going to color it blue. But it was still the choice I made that eliminated the possibility of another choice, not his knowledge of the choice I was going to make. Before I acted I could have chosen any of several colors. His knowledge of the choice I would make played no role in determining my choice or in eliminating other possibilities. This is what I mean when I

---

[24] What I am saying may reflect the distinction I mentioned in footnote 11 between absolute and suppositional necessity. What I state as logically impossible is perhaps, from God's perspective, suppositional necessity. But I have no desire to pursue that explanation or use that terminology. David Hunt, "A Simple-Foreknowledge Response," 75, says that medieval thinkers called this "accidental necessity." I still like "certainty" better.

say that speaking of an event as foreknown puts us logically on the other side of the event. The "cannot" results only from the assumption up front—if God knows I am going to color it blue—and so is only a logical "cannot," not a statement of ability, not an ontological "cannot."

In other words, then, it is fine to say that if I am going to make a given choice tomorrow, I cannot make a different choice. Of course! But it is the protasis of that conditional statement that means I cannot, not some divine knowledge or decision undergirding that knowledge that limits my freedom. When the time to choose arrives, I can make any choice that is at my disposal. If, however, I can make only the choice I make, as a matter of ability rather than logical exclusion, then I have not freely chosen. In fact, nothing about God's foreknowledge produces that effect.

Second, when we pose a situation where a choice is made, we place ourselves, logically, on the other side of the choice. From that vantage point, with the choice settled, the other choice is no longer logically "possible." Any choice already made cannot be a different choice, but at the time I made the choice I could have made a different one.

The same response is appropriate for observations like this one: If I choose differently from the way God knows I will choose, that will make him mistaken. No, the point is that if I choose differently God knows that. I cannot make choice A when God knows (whether before or after) that I am making choice B—or if anyone else knows this. Logically, then, I cannot choose differently from the way God knows I will choose, because his knowledge depends on my choice. He only knows the choice I will make as a result of the fact that I will make that choice.

Questioning this relationship is a self-constructed, logical dead end, an absurdity. The point is that until the future occurs, it has not yet happened. To be sure, I cannot make (using "cannot" for logical possibility again, rather than for ability) a choice other than the one I make. But that is clearly not the same thing as saying that I have to make the choice I make. When I really am free and able to make either of two choices, it is still true that if I go one way I cannot go the other. And there is no mystery, nothing significant, in that realization.

All such conundrums—if that is what they are—exist only because we forget we are speaking, logically, from the other side of the choice. Indeed, God's foreknowledge of our choices represents "seeing" them from the other side. Knowledge of a fact, for God, is logically after the fact, even if it is before the fact temporally.[25]

Conclusion

To put this into the context of this book, the point is again that we simply do not know quite how to view the relationship between God in eternity and God in the real world of space and time. The next chapter will offer a more speculative possibility for understanding this mystery, but the solution offered in this chapter, being the real solution, is the only one we need.

Foreknowledge belongs to God in eternity. Observing Abraham's obedience or Nineveh's repentance belongs to God in space and time. Abraham obeyed and Nineveh repented in the time-and-space world that God created and is active in. And, yes, God (fore)knew in eternity that both of those things would take place, just as he knew all the factors that went into their decisions and that they could have chosen differently.

The key consideration, however, is this: whatever God knew and decided in eternity, he knew and decided in consideration of what Abraham and Nineveh actually did in time. His knowledge of that did not determine their choices. Their choices were determined in real time and space in the very way such choices are determined, in the very way the biblical record depicts them—self-determined, that is.

---

[25] The question remains whether one can speak of anything as temporally before or after for God. Nonetheless, he knows very well the temporal relationship of all events in time and space, and his knowledge of them at any time in the temporal world before they actually happen (like yesterday, for example) is foreknowledge. Furthermore, he is able to intervene at any point in the sequence of events. All things past, present, and future may be "present" to—known to—God at the same time, but even if they are, he perceives them in their temporal and spatial loci and relationships. Otherwise, he would know even less than we do about them.

Deterministic theologians who disagree do not really disagree because of God's foreknowledge if it is considered strictly as knowledge. They disagree because they have an entirely different view of how God and human beings interact. As I have been suggesting all along in this book, determinists are so committed to an a priori, metaphysical view of God as the one who determines all things, that they must view all the biblical accounts of the interaction between us and God in a way that makes all human choices necessary, not free. For them, foreknowledge includes foreordination.

I urge all who consider such matters: it is time to give up using foreknowledge as an argument against freedom. That argument fails to persuade, at least in part because it is not the real argument, which is determinism itself and the arguments for determinism. Nor is God's sovereignty an argument against human freedom. God's sovereignty requires only that the world operate as he has designed it to operate. If he has designed the world so that all human actions have been made necessary by virtue of his foreordination, the world will operate that way, under his sovereign government. If, on the other hand, he has designed the world so that many human actions are free, this is the way the world will operate, under his sovereign government.

The question, then, is this: Is the world operating deterministically or with libertarian freedom? The answer depends on the teaching and interpretation of Scripture, not on arguments from foreknowledge.

Paul Helm's Argument from Foreknowledge against Human Freedom

In his work *Eternal God*, Paul Helm argues that God's foreknowledge and libertarian freedom are incompatible. This freedom he also calls "indifferent freedom," "agent-causal freedom," or "libertarian freedom"—and at least once "free will" (cited below); "libertarian freedom" is probably the phrase most commonly used by theologians and philosophers in discussing the matter. For the sake of convenience, in this excursus, I am going to represent libertarian freedom simply as "freedom," although I readily acknowledge that determinists like Helm affirm that humans possess a "freedom" of sorts, defined in compatibilist terms.[1]

In other words, Helm is saying that if an eternal and immutable God has foreknowledge of human beings' choices, then they cannot possess libertarian freedom.

---

[1] Simply put, compatibilism touts freedom to do only what one does and denies the freedom of alternative choice.

Helm's Two Concepts of Foreknowledge

To begin with, Helm distinguishes between two concepts of foreknowledge, which he calls O-foreknowledge and A-foreknowledge.[2] This sounds like two kinds of knowledge, but it means two different ways, among theologians, of conceiving of or defining foreknowledge, two views as to what foreknowledge entails.

The first of these two, O-foreknowledge, I will refer to as "noncausal foreknowledge." This way, foreknowledge of something future will be known as true for no reason other than the fact that it will occur.[3] If God has A-foreknowledge of something, however—which I will refer to as "causal foreknowledge"—he foreknows that it will occur because he has foreordained or otherwise made necessary its occurrence.[4] This matches what I have said regarding those who conceive of foreknowledge as something more than mere knowledge, investing it with the character of foreordination.

Helm concedes in effect, but with qualifications, that his argument against human freedom from foreknowledge only holds if foreknowledge is A-foreknowledge (causal foreknowledge), acknowledging that perhaps mere O-foreknowledge can coexist with libertarian freedom.[5]

Thus, my view of foreknowledge as not causal (O-type) is different from Helm's. In light of his concession, the discussion of Helm's views might end here. Nevertheless, for two reasons I will proceed to consider

---

[2] Helm, *Eternal God*, 128–42 (see chap. 1, n. 5).

[3] Helm, 131. He often represents foreknowing as knowing the truth of propositions about the future. I will discuss the issue of the mode of God's foreknowledge in a later chapter. Meanwhile, I will avoid his manner of expression as much as possible without misrepresenting him. I am not convinced that foreknowledge is merely knowledge of the truth of propositions about the future.

[4] Helm, 128.

[5] Helm, 142. Subsequently (143–44), he reaffirms that A-foreknowledge is not, and O-foreknowledge is, compatible with libertarian freedom. This is self-evidently true; if one defines foreknowledge to rule out human freedom, then the two are incompatible.

his arguments that divine foreknowledge and human freedom cannot be compatible. One reason is that he has qualified his admission that O-type foreknowledge might be reconciled with libertarian freedom in such a way that it is obvious he thinks the person who holds to noncausal foreknowledge will not be willing to meet the qualifications. The other reason is that it also seems likely that he really believes his arguments against freedom will prevail regardless of whether one regards foreknowledge as noncausal or as fraught with foreordination (causal). One reason for saying this is that he presents his argumentation in careful detail, and at length, well before he introduces the distinction between two concepts of foreknowledge.

Helm's Arguments against Foreknowledge

Helm affirms that if an eternal and immutable God has foreknowledge of human choices, it is not logically possible for human beings to have (libertarian) freedom. In a chapter titled "Timelessness and Foreknowledge," he provides two main arguments to sustain this particular affirmation.

Argument 1

The first argument, in Helm's words, is this: "If God knew yesterday that Jones will perform a particular action at some time in the future then God's knowledge is past. Being past it is unchangeable, and so necessary."[6] This argument—that foreknowledge is past (from the perspective of the time of the thing foreknown) and cannot be changed, is important for Helm, and he repeats it often, insisting that not only is God's foreknowledge past, unchangeable, and necessary, the event foreknown is equally necessary and therefore not free.[7] He explains that since God knew in the past what would occur today, the power of free choice would entail the power to change the

---

[6] Helm, 97–98.

[7] Helm, 101. See, again, 105.

past, which is impossible on its face; he adds that "God's foreknowledge of Jones's action 'secures' its performance."[8]

This argument is unconvincing. Although couched in different terms, the logic is exactly the same as the argument mentioned earlier, that if God knows what I will do I cannot do differently because that would make God mistaken.

Stated more simply, and letting the letter x represent a certain action, Helm's argument is this: if God foreknew in the past ("past" from my perspective, he means) that I will do x tomorrow, then the past cannot be changed and it is therefore necessary that I do x tomorrow and cannot do y instead. However, once the terms are carefully analyzed, this argument reduces to tautology.

The protasis, "If God knows I will do x," already entails that I will do x, since God would not know this if I were not going to do it. Thus the proposition says nothing more than "If I will do x, I will do x." Who can argue? Helm apparently accepts, correctly, that "What will be, will be" is tautology.[9] He should realize that "What God knows will be, will be" is effectively the same, unless "knows" means determines—and for Helm it does, thus showing that it is not foreknowledge that is incompatible with freedom but determinism. If I choose to do y instead of x, God would never have known that I will do x.

Helm is saying that God's knowledge, being prior to my choice, makes it necessary that I will do x since the past cannot be changed. At best, this can only affirm "necessity" in the sense of Aquinas's "suppositional necessity" (my "certainty"), which Aquinas illustrated by saying that if Socrates is sitting, it is necessary that he is sitting as long as he is sitting. Again, who can argue? "Certain" would be a better word than "necessary" for Helm to use for this kind of necessity, and then the statement would be true, even if tautological—and readers would not be confused or misled. If the word *necessary* is used, it can be nothing more than the "logical" necessity of affirming

---

[8] Helm, 97–98.

[9] I say this because he says Peter Geach does not view it as tautology, apparently implying that Helm himself does. Helm, 119.

that two contradictory things cannot both be true in the same sense. Such necessity is not an ontological necessity that means I have to do x for some reason other than my free choice. Whether I will do x freely, or because I can do nothing else, it is still true that I will or will not do x tomorrow—and that God knows which I will do. Furthermore, his knowledge, though it cannot be falsified, is grounded in what I will do, not vice versa.

Logically speaking, then, even a choice freely made, if it is foreknown by God what that choice will be, will certainly be what he knows it will be. In the end, Helm's argument does not even address the issue of whether I will do x freely or deterministically, much less require that the latter is the case.

If Helm is to be successful in arguing against freedom, then, he must deny that God has the ability to know future choices freely made. He does in fact deny this, and this is the reason he can say that free choices would violate God's immutability by changing his knowledge.[10] But to establish this will put the argument on an entirely different basis, one that is easy to affirm but impossible to defend. I, for one, am not willing to say that God cannot foreknow the choices of human beings made in libertarian freedom. Indeed, as indicated earlier, I see no reason to think he cannot.[11]

Indeed, Helm needs to make a coherent argument, one that is more than mere claim, that future free choices of human beings are ipso facto things that the infinite God does not have the ability to know. The argument he actually makes can be reduced to this: God cannot know future free actions because there are no such actions to know, because if he foreknows any action, it cannot be other than what he knows and is therefore

---

[10] Helm, 92.

[11] Helm, 125, correctly notes that his denial of the compatibility of libertarian freedom and God's foreknowledge exempts him from having to grapple with explaining how God could foreknow free human choices. He adds that those who do have this problem tend to favor "middle knowledge" as a way of resolving the issue. He is wrong about me, at least, and others whom I know. Furthermore, there are many who are not "current" theologians who affirm that God can know free choices and do not rely on "middle knowledge" to support their view, including Arminius and older Wesleyan theologians such as Richard Watson. (I will discuss middle knowledge in a subsequent chapter.)

necessary, not free. This argument is circular and tautological. In the end, it seems clear that Helm believes God cannot know anything that God himself has not predetermined, which brings us back to A-foreknowledge.

The preceding paragraphs answer Helm's first argument. I will return to observations along this line below, but first I give brief attention to his second argument.

Argument 2

Helm's second argument for the incompatibility of foreknowledge and human freedom is along these lines: divine foreknowledge is a timeless, "cognitive state"; consequently, "nothing can happen, now or at any time, to alter God's cognitive state."[12] The reason for this is that to alter God's cognitive state would violate his immutability.

Although this is couched in terms different from the first argument, it depends on the very same logical move. In that regard, then, this is essentially the same as the argument treated in the body of the chapter: one cannot act differently from the way God foreknows since that would make his foreknowledge mistaken.

The technical difference, here, is that Helm is focusing on God's timelessness and immutability. Even so, it is God's "cognitive state" that cannot be changed, and that refers to his knowledge of the future. In the first argument what was "past" was God's knowledge of the future: his "cognitive state," in other words. In the second, what is "timeless" is God's cognitive state: his "(fore)knowledge," in other words. Thus the two arguments depend on the same logic.[13]

Again, then, we meet tautology. God's "knowledge of our future" is knowledge of everything about our future that actually will be, so it is not possible for God to be mistaken. To say, then, that nothing can happen

---

[12] Helm, 105–6.
[13] I think it possible that Helm did not mean this as an entirely different argument but as another way of stating the same argument. I was not sure.

to alter that knowledge—that "cognitive state"—is simply to affirm in the predicate what the subject already entails. Yes, to change God's knowledge would mean that God is not immutable or omniscient, or even always right, which is impossible by definition. Thus, it is impossible to do what is impossible to do: to make any changes in what God knows or to falsify his knowledge, once we recognize that all his knowledge of the future is exactly what the future will be and derives from that future, else he would not know it. As already acknowledged, if I will choose x tomorrow, I will choose x tomorrow—and God knows it.

Further Observations about Helm's Arguments

Perhaps the similarity in the two arguments is the reason Helm devotes much less discussion to the second than to the first. Given that my responses would be essentially the same, I see no need to pursue this argument separately. But I will make several additional, relatively brief observations in the same connection, believing they speak to both arguments.

Helm holds that God's foreknowledge is what he calls A-foreknowledge, though he clarifies this later in his discussion. That is, what God foreknows derives from his own foreordination or predetermination of events. Well, then, of course if God has predetermined that I will do x tomorrow, I will necessarily do so—not because his knowledge of this choice was past from my perspective and the past cannot be changed, or because he is timeless and his cognitive state cannot be changed, but because God predetermined that I would do x. As the saying goes, this is "a horse of a different color." Such an argument ought not be conducted on the basis of foreknowledge but on the basis of foreordination.

If I do x today, it will not be God's knowledge of that fact that prevents my doing otherwise; it will be the fact that I do x that makes it logically (not ontologically) impossible for me to choose differently. To use the earlier illustration, if I will choose the blue crayon rather than the red one to color the ball, it is my choice that excludes the red as a logical possibility, and that serves as the grounds of God's knowledge that I will choose the blue.

In other words, when I say that if I choose the blue I cannot choose the red, I most certainly do not mean that I do not have the freedom and power to choose the red, and nothing in reality precludes me from choosing the red. Logically speaking, God's knowledge of my choice bears the very same relationship to my choice as when I say, "If I choose blue, I cannot choose red." When choice-time comes, I can choose any option open to me. That God knows what choice I will make logically entails that I will certainly make that choice but not that I will make it necessarily.

Helm's argument reduces to saying that it is not possible for people to choose in any way other than the choice they actually make because it is impossible for them to choose differently. Yes, it is impossible to change the past or to change God's cognitive state, but whatever choice a person makes is the choice that God has eternally known. God knows the future as it will actually be, so it is not possible for him to be wrong in the first place. Certainly, if God foreknows that I will do x today, then I will—but it would be better to say that if I will do x today, God foreknows that I will.

Helm observes that "if God knows all things, past, present, and future to us, that knowledge is unchangeable by anything which happens in time."[14] This is both correct and insignificant. "Anything which happens in time" is exactly what God knows; therefore, it is tautological to say that anything that happens in time cannot change anything that happens in time—or God's knowledge of it. Whatever has happened (or is going to happen) in time is what the omniscient God knows. That cannot then be turned into an argument about whether it happens freely or by foreordination. That is a different matter altogether.

To this he adds that nothing can possibly falsify anything in God's omniscience.[15] Well, for sure. And the reason we can say this is that he only believes what is true and only knows as true what actually will happen.

Surely determinists do not think that I or others holding to human freedom think anything like what the following imaginary scenario contains.

---

[14] Helm, *Eternal God*, 126.
[15] Helm, 126.

Let's see, I think I will go do x. But wait! God knows I am going to do x. Therefore, I am going to play a trick on him and make his knowledge wrong. Instead of x, I am going to do y. That will be fun! I will prove the theologians wrong and God in error.

No, whatever I am finally going to do, that is what God knows I am going to do—which proves nothing except the perfection of his knowledge. It will never be possible to make God's knowledge of what we will do wrong. If I am going to do y instead of x, God will never have known that I will do x. He can only know that I will do what I will do. Indeed, even if God suddenly lost his mind and no longer knew what I will do, I will still do exactly what I will do. Everything in the future is certain, and this includes free choices.

Those who participate in such discussions as this should beware: any time a sentence begins with "If [so and so] is true" the certainty of it has already been assumed, and all supposedly logical implications of such a protasis rest on that assumption. The same goes for a sentence that begins, "If God knows [so and so]," since ipso facto what God knows to be so is true—not said to be true because he knows it, but said to be true in that it is true. The words, "If God knows I will do x" have no logical force different from simply "If I do x."

Helm cites Peter Geach as saying, "If it is true at some later time that Johnny will die of polio, then nobody ever was able at some earlier time to bring it about Johnny was not going to die of polio. And this of course we do not believe: Johnny could have been preserved by a suitable injection, but his foolish parents neglected the precaution."[16] But Geach is mistaken: we do believe that "if it is true that Johnny will die of polio," no one ever could change that. Once the truth of something is assumed—in this case stated outright—nothing at any time can change it logically. Again, we have a subtle tautology, like that contained in "What will be, will be."

---

[16] Peter Geach, "The Future," *New Blackfriars* (1973), 211, cited in Helm, *Eternal God*, 119.

Yes, if Johnny had been inoculated against polio he could have avoided death by polio, but in that case it never would have been true—or known to God as true—that Johnny was going to die of polio. It can only be known, by God, or anyone else, that something will be true if indeed it will be true.

Conclusion

Helm's argument attempting to prove determinism based on foreknowledge fails. His own acknowledgment that his argument might not hold against what he calls O-foreknowledge (noncausal foreknowledge) is telling. A prior commitment to determinism is at the root of his rejection of freedom. His use of foreknowledge as though it were yet another argument is misleading.

If we start our theological explanation of events with God's foreknowledge, we put ourselves on the wrong footing and we may choose a deterministic explanation. Instead, we ought to probe the things that take place in time and space in light of their own relationships, as signaled in the biblical record. Then we can speak of God's foreknowledge in a way that allows for everything involved in the events in time.

EIGHT

More about Foreknowledge
in Eternity and Time

The solution to the apparent problem of foreknowledge and freedom, in the preceding chapter, is adequate and correct as it stands. At the same time, some further considerations may prove helpful. The suggestions I offer here will not substitute for that solution or point in a different direction. They may, however, add a dimension to and shed an illuminating light on the way we view the problem.

The Element of Mystery

As indicated earlier, some of the apparently logical implications of God's eternal perfections may not mean what they seem to us to mean. God's infinite perfections are not entirely comprehensible to finite human reasoning, and these include some of God's attributes like incorporeality, impassibility, and immutability. Foreknowledge, though not technically an attribute of God except as included in his omniscience, works in a similar way.

If the logical implications we draw from God's foreknowledge appear to contradict the freedom we experience, and that is presented in the Bible, we need only to question not foreknowledge itself but the implications we have drawn from it. The Bible clearly teaches that God has foreknowledge. It also describes the real world he created as the context for our existence and God's interaction with us. The two things must, by design, be compatible.

While there is the appearance of tension between the immutability of God, for example, and the fact of creation, we do not have to decide between the two. God is absolutely and eternally perfect and complete in himself. He does not change. Even so, the temporal world we live in did not exist before he created it. Furthermore, this temporal world is real, and the unchangeable God interacts with us in it—in the ways Scripture depicts. In some way, then, there is a real "contact" point between eternal immutability and the temporal world. That fact is clear enough, but explaining or comprehending it is a mystery.[1]

In the same way, we do not have to choose between foreknowledge and the human freedom involved in the contingencies described in the Bible, contingencies that are commensurate with our experience. Even if we cannot explain how the two work together, we can accept the reality of both and leave a final resolution to the infinite God whose ways are past finding out (Rom 11:33). Our logic is no more infinite than our other abilities, nor has it escaped the noetic effects of sin. We do well to remember Ps 131:1: "LORD, my heart is not proud; / my eyes are not haughty. / I do not get involved with things / too great or too wondrous for me."

Divine foreknowledge means that God knows events before they occur. That much seems clear, even though the limitations of our reasoning show up when we say it. We simply do not know how to measure before when discussing the relationship between the eternally unchanging God and the

---

[1] By these comments, I do not intend to relegate all theological, or even philosophical, thinking to the realm of mystery. Mystery is something of a last resort, to be used when we have done our best with revelation, reason, and experience and encounter truth that exceeds their boundaries.

always-changing, temporal world of which we are part.[2] While the Bible itself speaks of things existing "before the foundation of the world," we are aware that, logically speaking, there was no before the creation of the world. Still, the world was not eternal. An eternally unchanging God has no before and after. When we reach that point in our thinking, we would be forced into silence were we not too proud to say nothing.

Some theological giants have attempted to explain such things. Thomas Aquinas, for example, apparently affirmed that all things are eternally "present" before God, that he consciously inhabits an "eternal now."[3] Without challenging this, I wonder if any finite human being, including Aquinas, can possibly understand what such an affirmation actually means.[4] We are time-bound beings, experiencing the flow of change at all times. For us to think or speak, as well as to act, is to change. We are not equipped to understand a radically different order of being.

Surely the God who created this space-time world knows even better than we the difference between one day and another, knows what has and has not yet happened. The biblical narrative is grounded in the view that he both understands the contingencies involved in temporal developments

---

[2] As Steven Lewis observed to me, our difficulties result in large part from the "limitation in our ability to talk about such relationships as God and time without using temporal language." Thus my observations in the first two chapters of this volume. Add to this the problem of the noetic effects of the fall.

[3] Aquinas, *ST* 1.14.13: "All things that are in time are present to God from eternity, not only because He has the types of things present within Him, as some say; but because His glance is carried from eternity over all things as they are in their presentiality."

[4] Brian Leftow, for example ("Eternity and Simultaneity," 164–68 [see chap. 1, n. 6]), observes that from God's frame of reference all events in time and space are simultaneous, whereas in the temporal frame of reference of the created world they are instead sequential or successive, noting that "the occurrence of things in eternity with God, which He perceives there, is the very occurrence by which they occur in time." Surely he does not mean this to be gibberish, but no one should be expected to understand it. There is every reason to think that the God who created time and space perceives this-worldly events as sequential, that in eternity he is aware of events as they they really are. This world is real.

and can intervene at any point in the sequence of events. The eternal Logos became flesh (John 1:14) on a specific day in history and "tabernacled"— erected his tent—among us. This was a date that actually can be pinpointed even though we do not have all the information needed to do so. The world we inhabit—the world God made for us—has past, present, and future, and God understands it and interacts with us in it, not just in eternity when there was no such world. Even God can say, as cited earlier, that he was angry with Israel for forty years.

To say these things is in no way to deny God's exhaustive foreknowledge, but to affirm the reality of the world of contingencies that he created and that Scripture describes. He knows what I am going to do in advance, but whether we can logically explain it, his foreknowledge does not mean that I am never able to make any choice different from the one I make, thus eliminating contingencies—and freedom—entirely. We must accept both that the choices we will make are certain and that we can make different choices. Contingent events mean exactly what they would mean if God did not know them. The biblical narrative requires us to take the choices described there to mean just what the record indicates they mean.

There will inevitably be an element of mystery, then, in our understanding how an eternal and immutable God, with his knowledge of all possible worlds, including exhaustive foreknowledge of everything that transpires, can function in a real world of time and space where all the events have the meaning ascribed to them.

A Speculative Possibility for Viewing This Tension

At risk of violating my own cautions, now, I offer as a possibility a speculative framework for expressing and viewing what appears to be tension between God's foreknowledge and human freedom. The reader will understand that speculative theology is not my first choice. I have taken pains to say, so far, that our finite theologizing, our speaking about God with its speculation and logic, is not entirely up to understanding or expressing the infinite and immutable God. This does not completely rule out speculative theology, but it does require that one acknowledge when one is speculating.

Speculatively and cautiously, then, I suggest that there must be some reconciling of time and eternity, some point of contact between a God who exists eternally without a shadow of change and a world of time and space and human beings in his image who make choices and are not puppets. Words to express this are inadequate, but here, before explanation, is the summation: there must be some coincidence, some intersection, between God's decisions and knowledge in eternity and his acts in time and space.

At the very essence of this suggestion, however, is the fact that the nature of this intersection or coincidence cannot be explained or comprehended by us. Here is mystery. I cannot define this intersection or explain how it can be. That we are not yet creatures in the eternal realm, but bound now to space and time, means that there is no way to represent precisely the relationship between eternity and time.

Even so, there must be a relationship, else God in eternity could not have created time and space and the cosmos that are bound in time and space. Without a point of contact, God the Son could not have entered our world. There has to be some intersection or coincidence, some identity perhaps, between the eternal state in which God alone exists as eternal and unchanging, and God's active creation of the space-time continuum we call the cosmos. If there were not some way of relating time and eternity, as unknowable (by us) as that way is, creation would not have been possible for God—not to mention the incarnation and his ongoing acts of sustaining and providentially governing the created world. God, in his unchanging eternity, can speak into existence, out of nothing other than his own will-power already existing, a world with "an evening and a morning, day one," with many days to follow.

There is no way such a thing as that can be, or that we can "make sense" of it. But there it is! In some way there was a connection, an intersection, a coinciding of eternity and time, a means of contact between them. That we do not know how that can be means, simply, that we do not understand eternity. We can affirm it, of course, but that does not enable us to define it or to say how eternity relates to a temporal world. To clarify, I am saying that there must be such an "intersection" (accepting this word only to represent a concept); I am not saying that I or anyone else can define or explain it.

To be sure, many have undertaken to define the relationship between eternity and time, but such attempts do not explain the way time and eternity intersect. They are of such radically different orders of being that no one can comprehend how they relate. The whole point of suggesting an intersection is that it can be affirmed, or at least proposed, but must remain a mystery.

"ET (Eternity-Time) Simultaneity" is one attempt to relate time and eternity and, briefly summarized, serves as an illustration why the attempt is doomed to fail. In this view, let eternity be represented by a horizontal fluorescent tube that is fully lit. Then let time be represented by another fluorescent tube parallel to the first, all dark except for one point of light that moves slowly along from one end to the other, representing the passage of time. Each point in time is simultaneous with the whole of eternity even though it is not simultaneous with any other point in time. In the tube of time, points are sequential. In the tube of eternity everything (including everything God knows) is simultaneous. Nothing there is before or after anything in time.[5]

Perhaps this attempt depicts some aspects of the relationship correctly, but it fails to elicit confidence. It is certainly flawed in some respects. For one thing, "simultaneous" is just as temporal a word as "before" or "after."[6] Eternity cannot be simultaneous with time, not even logically.[7] For another

---

[5] See Leftow, "Eternity and Simultaneity," 151–52. I have adapted his illustration.

[6] Davis, *Logic and the Nature of God*, 17–18 (see chap. 2, n. 4), makes the very same point.

[7] Helm, *Eternal God*, 27 (see chap. 1, n. 5), suggests abandoning the notion of simultaneity, saying: "Nothing time-free is simultaneous in any sense with anything which occurs in time" (32). Helm also notes the objection of Richard Swinburne to Aquinas's simultaneity, using the axiom that two things equal to the same thing are equal to each other: if an event today is simultaneous with eternity and a past event like the great fire of Rome is simultaneous with eternity, what happens today is simultaneous with the great fire of Rome; and this is nonsense. Swinburne

thing, it offers no way for the two realities to have a point of contact. We simply do not understand eternity well enough to relate it to time. We can affirm, however, an undefinable intersection between them in view of the eternal God's creation and sustainment of the space-time continuum and of his acts within and incarnation into the created order.

Genesis 28:12–13 may provide insight into such an intersection or contact point between eternity and the cosmos. Here is Jacob, heading for Haran both to escape Esau's vengeance and to obtain a wife. He arrives at the place he will subsequently name Bethel, House of God, and lies down to sleep. In his sleep he experiences a dream obviously sent by God.

In the dream, Jacob sees a ladder, with one end fixed to the ground and the other "reaching the sky," apparently reaching to heaven itself. The language is spatial, but any way of viewing the vision will lead to about the same meaning. Yes, it is a dream, but it at least represents a reality. Whether merely existential or fully real ontologically, angels are going up and down the ladder, back and forth from one (nonspatial) realm to another (spatial) one. And there "above it" (or "beside him"; we need not be crassly spatial) was Yahweh himself in heaven, speaking covenant promises (vv. 13–15) to Jacob on earth, promises for the real world and not just for the world of dreams.

At least in the dream, then, there was "intersection" between the eternal realm and the realm of time and space. Here were angels, coming and going between the two realms. Here was God in the eternal realm (eternally unchanging) speaking to Jacob in the world of time and space that is never still. If one could write a history of eternity—impossible by definition, no doubt—where would this event fit? How would it be told in that history? I suggest that it would have the same ontological meaning in God's eternity that it has in the biblical record of events in time and space. Should not we accept that the dream represents the reality of an intersection that can only be symbolized, not defined?

---

rejects God's timelessness. Swinburne, *Coherence of Theism* (Oxford, UK: Oxford University, 1979), 220–21, in Helm, 26.

Any number of incidents in the Bible might then be cited to develop this understanding. Having provided examples in chapter 5 of angels at work, I will add no more. All of them make plain that there is some kind of coincidence between the eternal realm, inhabited by the unchanging God and attended by his angels, and the always-changing world of time and space and human beings. The nature of an intersection between eternity and our world remains a mystery, but its existence seems certain.

The Value of This Suggestion

What, then, is the value of affirming that such an intersection exists? It enables us to think in a different way about the relationship between God's eternal purposes and foreknowledge and events in space and time. Theologians tend to think too narrowly about foreknowledge, while average Christians see foreknowledge as grounds for assurance that God knows everything and can be counted on to protect and guide us. A problem arises only when we think of foreknowledge as though it means the reality was in eternity and our present world is already fixed. No, the things that God foreknows about the future are not yet settled; they are settled in time and space—and in some way eternity coincides or intersects with that.

One helpful implication of this is clear: whatever an event in time and space means, metaphysically or ontologically, that event in the foreknowledge and decisions of God in eternity means exactly the same thing. In some way, God's foreknowledge of an event and the meaning of the event share identity.

It is wrongheaded to think of two "worlds"—God's knowledge in eternity versus events in the space-time world he made—as being so "other" that the "real" moments of space and time and the "logical moments" in God's eternal knowledge have different meaning. To think that way is to create a duality that is itself the problem.

For us to think in accord with that duality leads to something like the following. First, in God's eternity, which is at least logically "before" the foundation of the world, God has no beginning or end and exists forever without change. In that realm, God has all the knowledge and makes all the decisions. He predetermined everything. He knew all that would be because he ordained its existence and history, effecting his all-inclusive plan that made everything in the created world necessary.

Second, another realm entirely is the world of time and space, which began when God brought it into being, actualizing a world that did not previously exist except as he conceived it. In this world, which we human beings inhabit, events actually take place, as occasioned by divine or human action or by the natural forces that God set in motion at the beginning.

This duality then leads many theologians to conclude that the first of these two is of primary importance. Given that God is responsible for everything in the created order, including the apparently "free" actions of human beings, all the action in the second, temporal realm derives from God's decisions in the first, eternal realm. Thus everything in the world of time and space has been predetermined, settled in eternity. Every action in this arena is a necessary one, made so by God's eternal decisions.

More could be said to characterize events in the world of time and space in this view. But I say only that viewing the "events"—decisions and knowledge—of God in eternity and the events in time and space as though they belong to two distinct realms, with the eternal primary and the temporal having meaning only as settled in the eternal, is misguided and creates a problem.

Someone may object that we have no right to join the two worlds by positing that there is a coincidence or intersection between them. I suggest that others have no right to unjoin them. In the end, one way of viewing the relationship is probably no more speculative than the other.

Perhaps some things are easier for us to conceptualize if we maintain such a duality of realms in our logic. However, we should begin by conceiving of these two realms as one rather than as two, at least in how they speak truth to us. This is the reason for suggesting that there is coincidence or intersection between time and eternity, a shared identity. Definable or not, the coinciding is factual, as facts like creation, incarnation, and God's sustaining of the created order clearly imply. Furthermore, this way of viewing things has other important implications, regardless of how speculative the framework.

Primary among these implications is this: the fact represented by an event in time and the fact of God's knowing that event in eternity have exactly the same metaphysical meaning, the same ultimate reality, for theology. The two are not different entities in two different realms, with the latter being determined by the former. Instead, the two facts are one and the same fact, even if they are viewed from different perspectives. The Bible represents what God is knowing and doing in eternity and what he is doing in time as one story. Whatever meaning the event in history has, as pertains to divine-human relationships, for example, that same meaning applies to the event in God's foreknowledge of and purpose for it in eternity.

To put this in illustrative form, consider that Jonah goes to Nineveh to proclaim, as Yahweh has instructed him, that the city will perish in forty days. Hearing this pronouncement of judgment, Nineveh repents. Responding to their repentance, Yahweh forgoes the impending judgment he has declared. The meaning to be found in this account includes many things, but we may express an important aspect of it as influence and response. God genuinely plans—contingently—that he will destroy Nineveh in forty days, and he announces this. In response, the Ninevites make a free (libertarian) choice to repent. God, responding in turn, freely—and graciously—decides to withhold the judgment pronounced and previously intended.

Surely anyone reading the account without pre-formed, deterministic theological assumptions will correctly read it as having such meaning. Then when we view these events as things God foreknew and decided in eternity, we need to view them with exactly the same ultimate meaning. Since the acts in time are revealed, we should read the decisions in eternity in light of the revelation. His foreknowledge and decisions provided for the very influence-and-response interaction that the inspired narrative reveals.

We assuredly do not need to say something like, "Well, God foreordained (and/or foreknew) all this in eternity and so made it all necessary." Before time and space began, the all-inclusive providential government of God so fixed this that the Ninevites had to repent and God had to "repent" of his planned judgment. That way, the real world is the world of God in eternity, with the world of time and space as little more than a necessary reflection of it.

If we start with the biblical narrative, however, as set in the real world where God acts in the ways described there and interacts with humans in the ways indicated there, then our view of his knowledge and decisions in eternity is grounded in the view from earth and coincides with it.

Foreknowledge, then, need not mean anything different from what events in history reveal. Except, of course—and how significant this is—that God's foreknowledge speaks volumes about how he is at work to achieve his purposes and about the fact that all is going according to his overarching plan.

I can almost hear someone objecting: "But what about the fact that the Bible presents Jesus Christ as 'the Lamb slain from the foundation of the world' [Rev 13:8 NKJV]? Or 'He indeed was foreordained before the foundation of the world' [1 Pet 1:20 NKJV]? Was Jesus crucified before the world was created?"

To answer carefully but firmly, yes and no. Jesus was crucified in the world of time and space. If we had the information needed, we could pinpoint the exact date and place where the event transpired: somewhere in the outskirts of Jerusalem at a point in time within a very few years, one way or the other, of AD 30.

Is there a sense in which he was crucified in eternity? Yes, but only "in a sense." He was as good as crucified before the time of Gen 1:1, in that God planned for it, knew even then that the crucifixion would be needed, and decided that it would occur, incorporating everything involved into his all-inclusive plan—along with all the contingencies and influences that brought it about in time and space. There is substantial truth in affirming this, just as there is in affirming that God has eyes and ears, or that he feels joy and anger, or that he—though immutable—created the world of time and space when he had not created it forever.

In other words, our understanding of God's viewpoint is highly enhanced by speaking the truth from the vantage point of "before creating the world." This reassures us that the crucifixion was included in God's plan; it was not something that transpired out of his control or that thwarted his purposes. Nothing is out of his control or thwarts his purposes.

Even so, two facts do not change: (1) Jesus was crucified in time and space and not in eternity, and (2) all the meaning in his crucifixion in eternity coincides with the meaning of his crucifixion in actual history as revealed in the Gospels. There are not two meanings, here, with the eternal meaning being the decisive one. There is but one meaning here, and that is the one seen most clearly in the actual event in time and space as described and interpreted in God's Word. And "meaning" includes such things (and more) as whether the event was contingent or necessary, whether it was man's doing or God's—or both.

The certainty of Jesus's crucifixion in eternity is nothing more than the fact of his crucifixion in time. Any knowledge of that event is grounded in the event itself. God foreknew it (and planned for it) in that it actually happened outside Jerusalem as ordered by Pontius Pilate, who was procurator of Judea from AD 26/27 to 36/37. Thus we are not seeing two distinct events with two distinct meanings. There is one event, and it has one meaning in the eyes of God.

Foreknowledge is important, of course, and without question God eternally possesses exhaustive foreknowledge of all that happens in the universe. But understanding the true nature of foreknowledge helps us dispose of weak objections to freedom that are supposedly based on foreknowledge. Foreknowledge, as such, is not the effective grounds of any objection to human freedom.

In the following three chapters, I will treat some other matters involved in the theology of foreknowledge. This much seems clear already: God's foreknowledge of the future does not close the door to human freedom to choose in more than one way when faced with a decision. Even if one rejects the idea of an intersection or coinciding between time and eternity, other affirmations in this chapter and the previous chapter support that foreknowledge does not cancel libertarian freedom.

Conclusion

What happens in deterministic theology? Its proponents look at God's decrees and knowledge in eternity, on the one hand, and then at events in time and space narrated in the Bible, on the other. Instead of seeing an intersection, an identity of meaning shared by them, they build theology around the first and interpret the second to match. In effect, if not consciously, the question becomes, How can we view these events narrated in the Bible, when God is acting and interacting with us in time and space, in a way that will accord with what our theology tells us about God's decrees and knowledge in eternity?

This approach leads to questions and observations such as the following: (1) How can God act sincerely to try to persuade people to do right and avoid wrong when he knows (and has decreed) that they will do wrong instead? (2) How can man have libertarian freedom when God's sovereignty by definition means that he makes necessary all actions? (3) How can God possibly be sincere in dealing with people as though they have freedom when he has already "seen the movie"?

Such theology is wrongheaded. Here is what we ought to do instead. Yes, take a look at who God is in himself in eternity, including his eternal omniscience and decrees. Look also at his acts in time and space, both creating and then interacting with the created order and the humans he has placed in that realm. Then look at how he has revealed in Holy Scripture the way his interaction with humans has occurred and what it means. And then ask this instead: How can we view the decrees and knowledge of God in eternity in such a way that will match what revealed theology tells us about God and his acts in time and space?

The perspective thus gained will make a great difference in theology. Furthermore, that difference will be justified, since the biblical account of God's acts in time and space is far clearer and more detailed than its description of him in eternity or than our logical reasoning about who he is in himself. The world we live in is the real world he made to be the arena for his acts. This is where he reveals who he is and what his plan is and what he intends the world—including the world of human beings in his image—to be. Let the biblical record be the starting point of theology. Let theology define God in those terms and refine its view of God in eternity to match that.

NINE

Why Open Theism
Does Not Work

Some theologians have adopted open theism in order to solve the supposed problem that God's exhaustive foreknowledge is not compatible with human (libertarian) freedom. To accomplish this they deny God's
exhaustive foreknowledge. I have dealt with this, matter elsewhere but provide here a summary of key reasons for rejecting this view.[1]

Open theism is a relatively recent form of theology that has grown out
of what seems, at least at first glance, to be a kind of Arminianism. I prefer
to call it "neo-Arminianism." It is neither consistently Arminian nor faithful
to the theology of Arminius. It also contradicts traditional theism.[2]

---

[1] Picirilli, "Foreknowledge, Freedom, and the Future," 259–71 (see chap. 7,
n. 7); "An Arminian Response to John Sanders's *The God Who Risks, A Theology of
Providence*," 467–91 (see chap. 7, n. 7).

[2] Some similarities exist between open theism and process theology, but to
develop that would go beyond my purposes here.

The Nature of Open Theism

I tend to think of the 1975 publication of *Grace Unlimited*, edited by Clark Pinnock,[3] as the foreshadowing of this movement—although at that point most of what it contained was agreeable to traditional Arminian theology. (I assume that several of the contributors to that volume would not espouse open theism.)

A dozen years later, *The Grace of God, the Will of Man*—something of a sequel to the volume just named—appeared. [4] By this time, the denial of God's exhaustive foreknowledge had begun to take shape. In subsequent years, a number of volumes developed this view in greater detail.[5]

What is open theism? Primarily, it aims to represent God as one who is in a dynamic, interpersonal, give-and-take relationship with truly free persons whom he created in his image to love and win to himself without coercion. That much, many of us may appreciate.

But there is more to open theism. The most obvious problem is that these theists are agreed in denying God's exhaustive foreknowledge of the future. They insist that if God knows the future moral acts and decisions of human beings, that future is fixed and cannot be otherwise. Consequently, to believe in exhaustive foreknowledge, they say, sounds a death knell for a truly interpersonal relationship between God and humanity.

---

[3] Clark Pinnock, ed., *Grace Unlimited* (Minneapolis: Bethany Fellowship, 1975).

[4] Clark Pinnock, ed., *The Grace of God, the Will of Man* (Grand Rapids: Zondervan, 1989).

[5] Among those who shaped the movement, see Richard Rice, *God's Foreknowledge and Man's Freewill* (Minneapolis: Bethany Fellowship, 1985); William Hasker, *God, Time, and Knowledge* (Ithaca, NY: Cornell University, 1989); Clark Pinnock, Richard Rice, et al., *The Openness of God* (Downers Grove, IL: InterVarsity, 1994); John Sanders, *The God Who Risks: A Theology of Providence* (Downers Grove, IL: InterVarsity, 1998); Greg Boyd, *God of the Possible* (Grand Rapids: Baker, 2000); Clark Pinnock, *Most Moved Mover: A Theology of God's Openness* (Grand Rapids: Baker, 2001). See also Beilby and Eddy, eds., *Divine Foreknowledge* (see chap. 7, n. 17), in which Boyd defends open theism.

This denial of divine foreknowledge, by the way, is not only contrary to classic theism, but it also contradicts traditional Arminian theology. Neither Arminius nor evangelical Arminians have found it necessary to deny God's exhaustive foreknowledge.

For additional clarification, open theists agree that in the Bible God often speaks about the future. This can happen in any of three ways: (1) God may predetermine that he is going to do certain things unconditionally without regard to human cooperation, and may announce this in advance. For example, he knew—and shared with Noah—the fact that he was going to destroy the world with a flood. (2) God knows human beings and their present circumstances perfectly and can predict what they will do and speak reliably about the future—at least, usually. Jesus was able, in this way, to foretell Peter's denial of him. (3) Sometimes, when God speaks about the future, even at times when the biblical record does not say so, he is speaking conditionally rather than absolutely. For example, although he said to Jonah that he would destroy Nineveh, he meant—by implication, at least—that he would do so if those in Nineveh did not repent.

There are at least two important things about this view. First, it means that God is sometimes wrong, and the open theists frankly acknowledge the possibility. In spite of his thorough knowledge of human beings' hearts and circumstances, they do not always act as he would predict. In such instances, he will be surprised; he is, after all, vulnerable and can be hurt and disappointed.[6] He may sincerely expect a person to act in one way and find his expectation mistaken.

The second thing is that the open theists do not really believe that God knows the future. They agree that God exhaustively knows the past and present, a view sometimes called "presentism." Early in the movement, some of the open theists only denied that God knows in advance our free choices and actions. They called this "limited omniscience"—an apparent oxymoron.

---

[6] Kevin Hester sees some similarities between open theism and the theopaschite controversy in the early church.

Two things can be said about this. First, the free actions of human beings are so intricately interwoven with all the events of the history of earth and man that it is logically impossible for God to know any of the history to come if he does not know the choices that humans will make. Second, it is clear that when they speak of God's knowing some other aspects of the future, they do not mean foreknowledge as it has traditionally been understood. In none of the three ways that open theism says God may speak about the future is God actually "foreknowing" what lies ahead: not when he speaks conditionally, not when he speaks predictively and may be mistaken, and not even when he announces what he is going to do. In the last case, he is actually determining and declaring what will be; any knowing he experiences is entirely derivative.

Pinnock, for example, approvingly summarizes Rice as saying, "If human choices are truly free . . . they do not exist to be known in advance by any knower, even God."[7] Pinnock himself said, "Decisions not yet made do not exist anywhere to be known even by God."[8] But if future decisions do not now exist, neither does anything else in the future. So if God cannot know future free events because they do not exist, then God cannot know any future events.[9]

The Reasons Open Theism Fails

Open theism will not work for many reasons, and I have already suggested two: that it means that God can be wrong, and that it means that God does not really know the future at all. Beyond these and others are three important reasons.

1. Open theism will not work because it sets out to solve a problem that does not exist, accepting the faulty premise that the future cannot be known

---

[7] Pinnock, *Grace of God*, xii.

[8] Pinnock, 25.

[9] I will have a little more to say about God's knowledge of future contingencies in a subsequent chapter.

without being closed. This was the main reason the open theists denied that God knows the future, free acts of human beings. Rice wrote:

> In spite of assertions that absolute foreknowledge does not elimi-
> nate freedom, intuition tells us otherwise. If God's foreknowledge
> is infallible, then what he sees cannot fail to happen. This means
> that the course of future events is fixed, however we explain what
> actually causes it. And if the future is inevitable, then the apparent
> experience of free choice is an illusion.[10]

This is the primary reason open theism denies God's foreknowledge of the free decisions of moral beings. This does not work because it is a logical misstep, an entirely unnecessary move that assumes a faulty understanding of what it means for the future to be certain and knowable. To express this positively, there is nothing about the certainty of the future—and the fact that God knows it exhaustively—that is in conflict with the ability of human beings to make free, moral decisions.

In question form, the issue is simply this: Does foreknowledge close the future? It does not, as I argued in chapter 7. Arminian theologians, all the way from Arminius himself to the present day, have affirmed that God foreknows all events perfectly and that this in no way closes the future or eliminates human freedom in making choices in real time.

In light of the treatment of this in chapter 7, which focuses on the "problem" of foreknowledge and freedom, the arguments made there need only brief review. One thing required in this discussion is to make sure we clearly define the terms we use and not use them ambiguously. Of special importance are three terms: *certainty*, *contingency*, and *necessity*.

First, we distinguish between contingency and necessity. Necessary events are those that must be the way they are. They are caused by some force that makes any other result impossible. This may involve natural law, for example,

---

[10] Richard Rice, "Divine Foreknowledge and Free-Will Theism," in *The Grace of God, the Will of Man: A Case for Arminianism*, ed. Clark H. Pinnock (Grand Rapids: Zondervan, 1989), 127.

like gravity. Or it may involve the unconditional act of God: if the effect of his influence cannot be other than it is, the result is a necessity.

By contrast, a contingency is anything that really can take place in more than one way, depending on the decision of the persons acting. To be truly contingent, a choice must not be the inevitable or unavoidable result of either natural law or the necessitating influence of God. We often speak of such choices as the exercise of libertarian freedom. "Self-determinism" may be an even better name.

The term *certainty* is different; the certainty of any event—past, present, or future—means nothing more than its "factness" or "eventness": the fact that it is or was or will be.[11] It is certain that John F. Kennedy was assassinated, for example, on November 22, 1963, in Dallas. It is equally certain that Hurricane Katrina struck New Orleans on August 29, 2005. In both cases, the certainty of the fact is grounded in the fact itself. The events, before they occurred, were certain in that they were going to take place; afterward, they were certain in that they had taken place.

Now one of these two events was a necessity, reflecting natural law: the cause-and-effect events involved in producing the hurricane and its movement. The other was a contingency, reflecting a free, moral choice. No force outside himself made Lee Harvey Oswald mount the stairs at the Texas Book Depository and pull the trigger for the fatal shot. As facts of the past, both are certain to us knowers. Thus, certainty has nothing to do with whether an event is necessary or contingent; those two terms deal with the nature of an event, whether the product of a cause-and-effect relationship or of self-determination. Certainty has to do with the "factness" of an event, with whether it is.

The same is true for the future, as known to God. Intuitively aware of the future as it will be, God is certain about it.[12] But his knowledge of it does not cause it or rule out any other contingent possibilities. If a future event is a

---

[11] There may be (as I have said in an earlier note) some correspondence between my "certainty" and the "suppositional necessity" of Aquinas, but I do not press that point.

[12] I will discuss the actual mode of God's foreknowledge in the following chapter.

contingency, such as a free choice that can go more than one way, God knows as certainty whichever choice will obtain. In short, an event—including a future event—can be both certain and contingent at the same time. Certainty does not make the future necessary; it does not close the future. The future can be certainly known and still open.

The Spanish have a saying, "*Que será, será*," which means "What will be will be." (Doris Day made a hit of the 1950s song by this title.) Is it right that whatever will be will be? Yes, and the statement only sounds fatalistic. In fact, the statement is mere tautology, nothing more than "what will be = what will be." Of course. That is what certainty means.

Even for the future, then, the certainty and knowability of an event flow from the factness of the event itself, not the other way around. God's foreknowledge of a future event in no way causes it or eliminates other possibilities. Instead, his knowledge reflects the event simply as an event that will transpire.

This is the logical stumbling block that leads the open theists astray. They think they must deny foreknowledge in order to affirm contingency and human freedom. What they do not realize is that the future would still be certain even if God did not know it. Or if anyone else knew it. Or if no one knows it. The opposite of a certain future is not an uncertain future; it is no future at all.[13]

Open theism really does get this logically backward. John Sanders, for example, says that a God who knows that I am going to have an automobile accident cannot answer a prayer for protection from accidents, since if he took action to prevent it he would change the future and make his own knowledge wrong. So, Sanders says, a God with foreknowledge is worse off, not better; his hands are tied by his knowledge.[14]

Sanders has turned foreknowledge on its head. What he says is exactly the same, logically, as if I said that I know that Rocky Marciano retired as

---

[13] It may be, as Steven Lewis suggested to me, that the open theists' problem in this regard results from the fact that their denial of foreknowledge makes God subject to the limitations of time and so a temporally limited being.

[14] John Sanders, *The God Who Risks: A Theology of Divine Providence*, 2nd ed. (Downers Grove, IL: IVP Academic, 2007), 213–14.

heavyweight champion without ever losing a bout. And therefore, because of that, he could not have lost any of his fights because to do so would have made my knowledge wrong. The fallacy in that is immediately obvious and equally so for Sanders's objection. Had Marciano lost any fights, I would never have known that he would retire undefeated. And if God knows I am going to have an automobile accident, he knows it only if I am. No doubt this includes his own decision to work through all the contingencies involved (including anyone's prayers for me) in such a way as to allow that accident. Should he decide to prevent an accident he sees developing in a given set of circumstances, it will not change his knowledge; he knows both that the accident will happen if he does not intervene and that it will not if he does.

To summarize, the first reason open theism will not work is that the denial of foreknowledge involves a fundamentally flawed understanding of the relationship between the knowledge of an event and the event itself. Foreknowledge does not—neither logically nor biblically—close the future. To put this simply, God knows what I will do in the future only if I am going to do it. That knowledge says nothing at all about whether I will do it of my own free choice—although, of course, God knows that too.

2. Open theism will not work because it does not solve another of the problems it is designed to solve: the problem of evil. Open theists have thought it easier to deal with the problem of evil if they deny that God knew, when he created the universe and man, that we would bring sin and its consequences into his world.

Critics of Christianity have often lodged such objections to our faith. John Hick, for example, has said that it is "hard to clear God from ultimate responsibility for the existence of sin, in view of the fact that he chose to create a being whom he foresaw would, if he created him, freely sin." Sanders cites this and appears to agree, so he retreats to the position that God did not know that Adam and Eve, and all the rest of the human race, would sin.[15] And

---

[15] Sanders, 202.

thus the open theist thinks he has defused this objection and cleared God of responsibility for sin.

Sanders pursues a specific illustration of this point: the Holocaust.[16] In spite of a foolish denial by some, we are aware that Hitler and his minions executed millions of Jews during the World War II period. It was, indeed, heinous evil, something that can appropriately be used to symbolize the worst of all evils.

Some questions, then: Did a wholly good God recognize this as evil? Yes. Did he permit it to take place? Yes. Could he have prevented it? Of course. Why did he not do so, then? And here the open theist has the answer: because God did not know it in advance, else he would have been responsible to prevent it.

This explanation will not work for one simple reason. Even if God did not foresee the Holocaust before it transpired, he most certainly was aware of it early on. If he knew Hitler as well as the open theists say he knows us all, surely God discerned what Hitler was up to. God must have heard the orders Hitler gave to his officers. Who doubts that God saw the masses being herded into the cattle cars and railroaded off to Auschwitz, or the other killing places, and was aware of the ovens and gas chambers awaiting them there? When the first thousand were stripped and gassed, surely God recognized that there would be multiplied thousands more to follow. And yet he did not stop the slaughter.

If knowing the Holocaust in advance would have obligated God to prevent it, knowing it as it transpired likewise would have obligated him to stop it. Why did he not intervene? The critic's question remains just as hard for us as it did before open theists denied God's foreknowledge. The open theist, after all, has no better solution, no answer for the question why a good and all-powerful God allows evil.

Why did God not prevent, or not stop, the Holocaust? In the end, we do not know—except to say that he most certainly allows evil in his universe for reasons that, even if we cannot discern them, are finally good.[17] It may well be

---

[16] Sanders, 201.

[17] Helm, *Eternal God*, 142 (see chap. 1, n. 5), notes that determinists will say, with Augustine, that "evil exists for a good reason." We who affirm libertarian freedom can say the same thing, that such freedom provides at least one "good reason."

that the true answer at least involves God's decision to create free, moral agents who are capable of good or evil—and of a personal relationship with him.

Is this the best of all possible worlds? I do not attempt to answer that question, but when God had finished creating, including the first humans, he declared the creation "very good" (Gen 1:31). And then sin entered the picture, making possible all sorts of terrible things. Open theism does not work because it does not solve the problem of evil.

3. Open theism will not work because God knew before the universe was created that Jesus was going to be offered for sin, thus proving that God foreknew human sin, a fact that destroys open theism in its primary claim. If God knew, before he created human beings, that Jesus would die for their sins, he had to foreknow that they would sin.

The biblical picture is both important and pervasive: that the death of Christ as a sacrifice for our sins was part of God's eternal plan—and this is the sense in which Jesus died before the foundation of the world, discussed briefly in the preceding chapter. The following four passages demonstrate that God knew that Jesus would die for sin "before the foundation of the world."

1 Peter 1:18–20

Translated literally from the Greek, the verses say that we were redeemed "by means of precious blood as of a spotless and blemish-less lamb, Christ, foreknown before the foundation of the world." It is possible that the participle "foreknown" refers back to "lamb" or to "Christ," but this makes little difference. The main question is, What was "foreknown" about this lamb, Christ? Open theist Sanders insists that it was not Christ's death that was foreknown but his person, and that it was Christ's incarnation that was preplanned, not his atonement.[18] He has little choice; for an open theist, God could not have foreknown that the human beings he had decided to create would sin and need atonement.

---

[18] Sanders, *God Who Risks*, 101–2.

But the context seems clearly against this limitation. For one thing, the Christ "foreknown" here is the Christ as he is identified here. There are two identifying phrases: (1) he is the Christ who is "a spotless and blemish-less lamb," and (2) he is the Christ by whose "precious blood" we were redeemed. Surely this is part of what was foreknown before the foundation of the world; otherwise, the point of Peter's statement is severely blunted, if not entirely lost.

Even if we omit the reference to a lamb entirely, we are left with this: "We were redeemed by the precious blood of Christ, foreknown before the foundation of the world." His atoning death ("blood") is so closely involved that it surely must be included in the foreknowing.

Furthermore, even if we should arbitrarily put aside the reference to his blood, we would still have, "we were redeemed by Christ, foreknown before the foundation of the world." This affirmation means that he was foreknown as "redeemer," which must involve the foreknowledge of the human sin from which redemption delivers us.

Greg Boyd's approach is different from that of Sanders. He says, forthrightly, "It seems that the incarnation and crucifixion were part of God's plan from 'before the foundation of the world' (1 Peter 1:20; cf. Rev. 13:8). Hence, Scripture makes it clear that Jesus was not crucified by accident. Rather, he was delivered up and crucified 'according to the definite plan and foreknowledge of God' (Acts 2:23; see also 4:28)."[19]

Consequently, Boyd takes these passages to mean that the event was predestined, but not the players: "It was certain that Jesus would be crucified, but it was not certain from eternity that Pilot [*sic*], Herod, or Caiaphas would play the roles they played."[20] But that is beside the point and diverts attention away from big-picture redemption of the sins of the world to small-picture concerns about foreknowing the sins of Pilate, Herod, and Caiaphas. The very passages Boyd cites make clear that the crucifixion was foreknown as part of God's plan for the purposes of redemption. Then God had to know about the sin that made redemption necessary.

---

[19] Boyd, *God of the Possible*, 45.
[20] Boyd, 45.

Ephesians 1:3–7

In the passage just treated, a key phrase is "before the foundation of the world." That phrase occurs again in Eph 1:4–5, where we read, "For he chose us in him, before the foundation of the world, to be holy and blameless in love before him. He predestined us to be adopted as sons through Jesus Christ for himself, according to the good pleasure of his will."

Most readers will see this as referring to eternal election, regardless of the differences in their theology of salvation. Some Arminians will take it as corporate election; I believe it includes individuals.[21] Calvinists take it as unconditional; I take it as election of believers. Regardless, the fact remains that this is (1) an election of persons in union with Christ, and (2) an election to redemption from sin. Likewise clear, the election is "before the foundation of the world."

This means at least two things. First, it means that God foreknew sin before the foundation of the world, or else he would not have been concerned with redemption at that point. Second, it means that the redemptive work of Christ was planned before the foundation of the world, or else the election described here would not have centered around him.

Furthermore, v. 7 makes explicit that this election brings us "redemption through his blood, the forgiveness of our trespasses." "In him" we acquire this, and we were chosen "in him" before the foundation of the world. Again, then, the death of Christ as atonement for sin—"his blood," in other words—was foreknown before the foundation of the world.

Both Sanders and Boyd attempt to solve this problem by making this solely a corporate election. Sanders says, "It is the group—the body of

---

[21] For the view that election is only corporate, see William W. Klein, *The New Chosen People: A Corporate View of Election* (Eugene, OR: Wipf & Stock, 2015); Robert Shank, *Elect in the Son: A Study of the Doctrine of Election* (Springfield, MO: Westcott, 1970); for the view that election is individual, see F. Leroy Forlines, *Classical Arminianism: A Theology of Salvation* (Nashville: Randall House, 2011), 121–28, 181; Picirilli, *Grace, Faith, Free Will*, 51–52 (see preface, n. 4); Roger E. Olson, *Arminian Theology: Myths and Realities* (Downers Grove, IL: IVP Academic, 2006), 181.

Christ—that is foreordained from the foundation of the world"[22]; Boyd says that "*whoever chooses* to be 'in Christ' is predestined to be 'holy and blameless before him in love.'"[23] Both of them seem not to realize that this is beside the point: if there was no sin foreknown when God made this election, there would be no election, not even corporately, of a "group" to be in Christ, for there would be no need for redemption by Christ.

2 Timothy 1:8–11

In vv. 9 and 10 Paul says that God "has saved us and called us with a holy calling, not according to our works, but according to his own purpose and grace, which was given to us in Christ Jesus before time began." Perhaps all will agree that this last phrase, "before time began," means essentially the same thing as "before the foundation of the world"; the NASB and NEB render, "from all eternity"; the NIV and TEV "before the beginning of time."

Then God's grace was given to us in Christ before time began; surely the participle "given" refers specifically to "grace." Its feminine accusative singular form is in agreement with that noun. The "grace" referred to here can be none other than saving grace, and that means that the recipients' sin was also known. It follows directly, then, that God saw sinful humankind's need for grace before humankind was created and determined even then to make us a gift of that grace in Christ. This provision necessarily implies Christ's atoning death as the basis for the gift of salvation by grace.

Again, Boyd tries to blunt the force of these words by making this a corporate gift: "Indeed, as a group we were given this grace 'in Christ Jesus before the ages began' (2 Tim. 1:9)."[24] But the gift of grace foreknown must by definition be a gift for sinners, foreknown as such, whether conceived corporately or as individuals. Only sinners need the grace spoken of here.

---

[22] Sanders, *God Who Risks*, 102.
[23] Boyd, *God of the Possible*, 46–47 (emphasis original).
[24] Boyd, 47.

Revelation 13:8

Though indirectly, by contrast with the negative, this verse refers to people "whose names have . . . been written in the Book of Life of the Lamb slain from the foundation of the world" (NKJV). And there are enough references to this Book of Life elsewhere in the Revelation to show that it holds the names of those who are saved. In the end, those whose names are written there are the ones with access to the glorious city described in the final chapters (21:27).

Now, the syntax here is possibly ambiguous, involving the linkage of the phrase "from the foundation of the world." The phrase may be linked either with the verb "written" or with the verb "slain." In other words, the text may say that the Lamb was slain before the foundation of the world or that these names were written in the Book of Life before the foundation of the world. Perhaps open theists will read it as "written before the foundation of the world." But this finally makes no difference; by either reading, we have the death of Christ as atonement for sin foreknown before creation.

We need not quibble over the linkage. Either reading is possible. The English versions are divided on the point. The AV, NKJV, NIV, REB, and others connect the words with "slain." The CSB, NASB, NEB, RSV, ESV, and others read "written before the foundation of the world." The same can be said for the commentaries: some link the words with "written" and others with "slain."[25]

So let us proceed as if the phrase goes with "written." If the names of the saved were written in the Book of Life from the foundation of the world, that means that God foreknew who would be saved. And if he foreknew that some would be saved, he likewise foreknew the sinful condition from which they needed to be saved, else their salvation would be meaningless.

---

[25] R. H. Charles, *Revelation*, ICC, 2 vols. (Edinburgh: T&T Clark, 1989), 1.354, links it with "slain"; James Moffatt, "The Revelation of St. John the Divine," *The Expositor's Greek Testament*, vol. 5 (Grand Rapids: Eerdmans, 1951) with "written"; both are confident of their reading.

Once we deny divine foreknowledge of the fall, as a fact, there cannot logically be any eternal knowing on God's part that some will be saved, whether a group or individuals. If he cannot foresee sin, he cannot foresee salvation from sin. If open theism is correct, there can be no book of redemption, written from the foundation of the world. It is difficult, then, to fathom that Boyd (who thinks in terms of corporate election, as indicated above) would acknowledge that "if any event was settled in the mind of God from the creation of the world, it was that the Son of God was going to be killed (Acts 2:23; 4:27–28; Rev 13:8)."[26] For Boyd to be consistent, this must mean that God did not know why he would be killed. I repeat: if the crucifixion was foreknown as sacrifice for sin, so was its redemptive purpose as deliverance from foreknown sin.

Furthermore, one notices that the very book in which the names were written from the foundation of the world is, in fact, "the book of the slain/ slaughtered *Lamb*." The slaughter of him for sacrifice was already, from the creation of the world, the basis for the existence of such a Book of Life. Indeed, the other references in the Revelation to "the (Lamb's) Book of Life" (3:5; 17:8; 20:12, 15; 21:27) include this idea by implication. The mere reference to Jesus as Lamb necessarily includes the idea that he was the sacrificial Lamb (cf. Rev 5:6, 12, for example, along with John 1:29).

It is clear, then, that Rev 13:8, regardless of how the words are read, means that the crucifixion of Christ, as the basis for redemption, was taken into account, as a fact, in God's planning, "from the creation of the world."

The four passages leave no doubt. They affirm that Christ as Redeemer and sacrificial Lamb was foreknown before the foundation of the world; that we, as believers, were chosen for redemption in Christ before the foundation of the world; that God gave us grace in Christ Jesus before time began; that before the foundation of the world, our names were written in the Book of the slain, sacrificial Lamb. Singly and together, the passages speak of definite

---

[26] Gregory A. Boyd, "The Open Theism View," in James K. Beilby and Paul R. Eddy, eds., *Divine Foreknowledge: Four Views* (Downers Grove, IL: IVP Academic, 2001), 31.

facts known as certain before creation. They demonstrate that the redemptive death of Christ as atonement for sin was eternally known and incorporated in the plan of God.

At this point, open theism is especially vulnerable, indeed invalidated, given that the position requires that God not foreknow the morally free acts of his creatures, especially the fall. The passages make clear that before he created the first humans, God both knew about our sins and knew his Son as our Redeemer by virtue of his death on the cross.

Conclusion

For at least three reasons, open theism's denial of God's exhaustive foreknowledge will not work. Its understanding of the relationship between knowledge and facts is logically flawed; its attempt to free God from responsibility for sin by affirming that he did not know about it is theologically flawed; and its failure to grapple with the clearly biblical teaching that God knew about the death of his Son as atonement for sin before the foundation of the world is exegetically flawed.

Open theism offers no help in understanding God's foreknowledge or its relationship with human freedom.

TEN

More Issues Related to
God's Foreknowledge

Other issues are involved in the theological discussion of God's foreknowledge. Some treatment of four of these is important for this work.

1. The Mode of God's Foreknowledge
and William Lane Craig

Some theologians appear to think that identifying the mode of God's foreknowledge may help mitigate problems that seem to inhere in the fact that
God knows everything that will happen in advance. Without being sure that
any theologians use the word *mode* to refer to this matter, I adopt the word
as appropriate for the discussion.

The question is how, or in what form, God knows the future. Perhaps
most of us tend to take for granted that this knowing is perceptual, although
most discussions of foreknowledge do not give this matter significant attention or use this terminology. Typically, we are likely to think that God sees
the future infallibly—although (as discussed in chap. 1) God has no eyes.

135

It is important to note that God's knowledge of the future is intuitive. Intuition, among other things, means "the direct knowing . . . of something without the conscious use of reasoning; immediate understanding . . . the ability to perceive or know things without conscious reasoning."[1] Among the key words here are *perceive, direct,* and *immediate.*

In other words, intuitive (fore)knowledge is perceptual, although not by any of the five senses. For that matter, God does not have our five senses, at least not the organs of those senses. Regardless, the perception involved in foreknowledge is mental perception. It is also direct, in that God does not arrive at this knowledge by any reasoning from one thing to another. He simply knows what I will do, for example, and not merely because he knows me well enough to predict what I will do; the ability to predict correctly is not foreknowledge as such. His foreknowledge is immediate, not mediated through any other processes, rational or otherwise.

A reader may think this discussion is pedantic, belaboring a point that is obvious. William Lane Craig and others, however, have offered that God's foreknowledge is not perceptual but conceptual,[2] referring to these two as different "models" of "divine cognition." He observes that the perceptual model "construes divine knowledge on the analogy of sense perception," which he considers "a terribly anthropomorphic notion." He explains that according to this model God "looks" and "sees" the future, which leads to the use of words like "foresight" to define foreknowledge. This model, he says, has problems "since future events do not exist" and therefore "there is nothing there to perceive."

By contrast, according to Craig, in the conceptualist model "God does not acquire His knowledge of the world by anything like perception." Instead, his knowledge is "self-contained, . . . more like a mind's knowledge of innate ideas." We should understand foreknowledge, then, to mean that

---

[1] *Webster's New World College Dictionary*, 3rd ed. (New York: Macmillan, 1996), s.v. "intuition."

[2] Craig, *Time and Eternity*, 264 (see chap. 3, n. 22), where also the rest of my quotations from him on this matter are found.

"God has essentially the property of knowing all truths," including truths about the future.

This issue may not draw major concern, but some attention to it seems warranted. The most important question about it is whether any of us can possibly know the mode of God's foreknowledge. Most certainly, we cannot learn this from Scripture, physics, or psychology.[3]

Craig's view requires that all of God's knowledge ("cognition") of the world of time and space, including humans and their actions, be conceptual rather than perceptual—which Craig would probably not take to be a criticism at all. But biblical language is most certainly perceptual, regardless of how anthropomorphic it is, as previously discussed in chapter 1. Furthermore, perception includes mental states as easily as sense-based brain states. Consider also Craig's observation that the future does not exist and therefore there is nothing there to perceive. In that case, one can as easily contend that there is nothing there to know.[4]

For another thing, this view inevitably means that what God knows about the future is not the future itself but "truths about the future." Such knowledge is, in fact, knowledge of the present statement about the future, not foreknowledge at all. This fact will also apply to the past, which likewise does not now "exist"—as Craig has acknowledged in the same book—and can therefore be known only conceptually.

I am not entirely persuaded, by the way, that God cannot know what does not exist, whether future or otherwise. Many believe God knows "all possible worlds," and only one of them actually exists. Romans 4:17b suggests that God speaks about such things, so he must know about them. But even without any such suggestion, I would not be bold enough to speak with confidence about God's inability in this regard. The fact that he knows the

---

[3] As David Hunt says, "I'm not at all sure how God knows the future, and I don't want my defense [of God's complete and infallible knowledge of the future] to be hostage to or dependent on a particular view on this subject." Hunt, "A Simple-Foreknowledge Response," 67 (see chap. 7, n. 17).

[4] For those who hold Aquinas's "eternal now" model of knowledge, our future is apparently present with God and thus fully knowable.

future means that he at least knows what does not exist yet. For that matter, I am not even certain what it means to say that the future does not exist.

Finally, the validity of the distinction Craig makes and of the implications he draws from it seems artificial. Be that as it may, especially significant in this regard is the fact that, whether by Craig's mode or mine, God knows what everyone is going to do in the future.

Consequently, for the purposes of this work, Craig's understanding of the mode of God's foreknowledge does nothing to alleviate the apparent problem between God's infallible knowledge of the future and the freedom of human beings to choose between alternative courses of action. Whether God's foreknowledge is conceptual, like self-contained and innate ideas, or perceptual, like "seeing ahead,"[5] God knows what the future holds, and if that contradicts human freedom, it is the fact of his knowledge that creates the problem, not the mode by which he obtained the knowledge or the form it takes in God's awareness. In truth, however, as shown in chapter 7, the problem lies in accepting the false premise that if God knows the future actions of a person, those actions are so necessary that the doer has no other choice. Anyone who thinks that advance knowledge is incompatible with human freedom will not be helped by conceiving of God's foreknowledge as conceptual rather than perceptual.

Happily, Craig himself does not accept that false premise. In a way very similar to that which I have set forth in the preceding chapters, he shows that "certainty" and "necessity" are not synonyms and that what will be is not the same as what must be. He correctly affirms that what God knows in advance will certainly come to pass, but this does not at all impinge on human freedom or remove the act from the realm of true contingencies.[6]

---

[5] "Seeing ahead" does not entail the caricature Craig draws of the perceptual mode as God's decision to "look and see" what the future holds. Intuitive foreknowledge is always with God direct and immediate.

[6] Craig, *Time and Eternity*, 256–58. My publication of this approach to the problem apparently predated Craig's. At least I was not influenced by him, or he by me. My thinking about certainty and necessity was at least in part influenced by Richard Watson, one of the earliest and best of the Wesleyan theologians; see

Among other helpful things, he notes, "We can be absolutely certain that *x* will come to pass. But it is muddle-headed to think that, because *x* will certainly happen, *x* will necessarily happen. We can be certain, given God's foreknowledge, that *x* will not fail to happen, even though *it is entirely possible that x fail to happen*."[7]

This clarification means that some claims about "problems" in foreknowledge are easily dismissed and need little discussion. Here are two such claims. (1) If God sees the future, then he has "already seen the movie." Apparently, this objection is supposed to create something ridiculous. (2) If God already knows how something will turn out, he cannot seriously labor toward a different outcome.

It is difficult to know whether to take such observations seriously; they are facile and shallow, if nothing else. For one thing, they are presumptuous, assuming we understand how foreknowledge works for God and implying that he cannot already have "seen the movie" without himself being affected in his relationship to the real world. Or that he cannot know how people will act without being discouraged from exercising persuasive influence on them. We simply do not know enough to know how God's foreknowledge affects him—other than to believe it gives him great advantage in determining just how to act. These claims are as misguided as those that say God himself cannot act to change the future he already knows, or that a person cannot act differently from what he or she knows since that would make him or her wrong.

For another thing, who can tell what motivates God to action? If he works to persuade someone to make a wise decision, all the while knowing that the person will decide wrongly, can he have no good reason for doing so? Perhaps attempting to persuade people to do right, regardless of how they are going to respond, is the right thing to do. Perhaps he needs to demonstrate his character and attributes, like his love or his justice. And perhaps he knows that the person really can decide differently.

Richard Watson, *Theological Institutes*, 2 vols. (New York: Nelson and Phillips, 1850), 1:375, 380.

  [7] Craig, *Time and Eternity*, 256–58 (emphasis added).

For yet another thing, "seeing a movie" is a very poor analogy for God's foreknowledge. It really is intensely perceptual, and it differs from God's foreknowledge in that what he foreknows is reality, in a time and space world he is acting in, not some depiction of it in a movie.

Furthermore, if he knows the reality of what transpires in time and space, that takes us back to the possibility, as suggested in chapter 8, that a metaphysical coincidence or intersection exists between eternity and time. Even if that speculative framework is not useful, it remains that God knows future events from the fact that they will occur, not before them in a sense that causes them.

Most important, however, is this: these objections are useless in arguing against human freedom because they add absolutely nothing to the problem of foreknowledge and freedom. Whatever view one takes of foreknowledge—what it means or how it is acquired or what form it takes—it means that God knows the future before it occurs. Then, regardless of the mode of that foreknowledge, God has that knowledge and the world works the way it does anyway. We are forced, in the end, to acknowledge that God is intelligent and self-conscious enough to know how to operate his universe sincerely and effectively in spite of the fact that he already knows how things will transpire. Once we realize this, we need only to rely on the logic I have set forth in chapter 7 to understand that his foreknowledge does not cancel human freedom.

Indeed, if one assumes a deterministic view of the way God operates his universe, the facile objections mentioned above will just as surely apply and verge on the bizarre. If his eternal decrees have made necessary all the choices that human beings make, he most certainly has "seen the movie," with whatever implications that fact is supposed to have. And he most certainly must labor with persons whose choices he not only foreknows but has already determined.

Ultimately, if God's exhaustive foreknowledge creates a problem for the view that humans possess libertarian freedom, any view that God knows the future creates exactly the same problem. If anyone attempts to defuse that problem by investing foreknowledge with the element of foreordination, the problem only grows worse. In that case God not only has seen the movie, he also wrote the screenplay—and directed it, and stars in it! That makes it even more difficult to grasp how he interacts with us in time and space, or how he labors to persuade persons who will certainly—and in that case necessarily—reject his advances.

2. The Mode of God's Foreknowledge and Paul Helm

In a way similar to that of Craig, Paul Helm thinks of foreknowledge as knowledge of propositions: "The future does not consist of events which are already occurring, but of sets of propositions which, because they are true, entail the happening of certain events. But these events are not occurring yet."[8] Helm is not alone in this; Stephen Davis, whose views are more libertarian than Helm's, defines foreknowledge as "knowledge of the truth-value of propositions about future states of affairs."[9]

To view foreknowledge in this way exclusively is not entirely satisfying. True, the future does not consist of "events which are *already* occurring"; who would ever have thought to say so? The future consists of events that will occur. Furthermore, to say that God's foreknowledge means that he knows the truth of propositions about the future (all possible ones, I assume) does not quite appear to be what is traditionally understood as foreknowledge. When Helm says that propositions are "true now," he unintentionally shows that knowing such propositions is knowledge of the present, not of the future itself.[10]

---

[8] Helm, *Eternal God*, 117 (see chap. 1, n. 5).

[9] Davis, *Logic and the Nature of God*, 52 (see chap. 2, n. 4). But see 65–66, where he seems to venture away from this definition in avoiding the implication that God foreknows some things inferentially rather than intuitively. He offers an interesting illustration of the difference between a computer's prediction of something ahead and "seeing" the future in a crystal ball, apparently preferring the latter as analogous to God's foreknowledge.

[10] Matt Pinson points me to the words of Watson, *Theological Institutes*, 1.421: "That the subject is incomprehensible as to the *manner* in which the Divine Being foreknows future events . . . even the greatest minds . . . have felt and acknowledged."

Perhaps a homemade illustration will convey the point. I am writing this on June 19, 2020. As I do I find myself in a context of events and circumstances. My cleaning lady has just left. I am about to take a break from this writing and get my lunch, and then I will see a doctor at 1:30 p.m. As I sit here writing this on my computer, I can see a very messy desk in front of me. My Bible and a copy of volume 5 of Aquinas's *Summa Theologiae* are immediately to my right on the desk, and even as I notice this, I feel a small resentment at the eBay bookseller who advertised the *Summa Theologiae* for sale for $19.95, used—but when it came it was only volume 5 of the *Summa*, a volume I have no use for, and the bookseller has not responded to my complaint of inadequate advertising. It could have been the one-volume edition, after all. My desk lamp is burning brightly; my old eyes need more light than they used to. On the wall to my left, a novelty clock—which a lady very dear to me, who is in a rehab facility, gave me for Christmas—has just sounded for noon with the call of a bald eagle. (There is a different bird call for each hour; I have to check the printed list—which I just did. I keep it on my desk to learn which call is which bird.) Off to my left is a Father's Day card that came in today's mail from my youngest daughter, who at this time is visiting in Missouri; I retrieved it from my mailbox when I came in from my morning walk shortly after my cleaning lady arrived.

All of this, and much more, is part of the context of my "present" in time and space. Yesterday, this entire set of circumstances was "future." It is difficult to believe that this "future" was then nothing more than a large number of propositions like the following. Bob Picirilli will be wearing khaki pants. He will have his hearing aids in and his glasses on. He will be writing these words in his computer, some of them during the period of 11:45 a.m. to 12:00 noon, on June 19, 2020. His cleaning lady will have left shortly before. His novelty clock will signal noon with the sound of a bald eagle's call. And so on.

Propositions are not reality. My present, yesterday's future, is reality in the world of time and space, not a set of propositions. God knows the future itself, it seems, not merely propositions about it. Being both omniscient and omnipresent, he is just as aware as I am—no doubt even more aware than

I am—of all these elements of time and space, fully conscious of all of it. He has direct and immediate access to everything existing everywhere at all times. And if this is true, in reference to the present set of circumstances for me and for God today, it was true for him yesterday—and at any time in earth's history past—in his foreknowledge.

A true proposition is one that "corresponds" to a state of affairs, in that it accurately describes and communicates that state of affairs to others; that is what propositions do. Even then, however, a true proposition is not the same thing as the state of affairs it describes. A proposition about my Bible is not my Bible. And a set of propositions about the future is not the future. Neither I nor God will be aware of my present as a set of propositions, and there is no good reason to think that he is aware of the future only as such. God always has direct access to the future. The object of his foreknowledge is the future itself. God knows the state of affairs that the proposition describes.

3. Knowledge of Counterfactuals

Lest some reader be put off by a term not already known to him or her, I begin by providing an informal definition of a "counterfactual." As the word itself indicates, it is a condition or set of circumstances contrary to fact. In other words, a counterfactual is an event different from the one that actually occurs. For example, using the illustration I used in chapter 7, let us say that yesterday, when I took my walk in the park, I took the left fork. Taking the right fork, then, is or was counterfactual.

We usually raise this question in discussions about the future, so let us say that tomorrow, when I take that walk, I will choose the right fork. God knows that I will (although I do not have to) and everything that will follow from that choice, like how long it will take to finish my walk, or whether I will encounter a rabbit along the way, or any of numerous other possibilities. To say that God knows counterfactuals, then, is to say that he also knows what would follow tomorrow if I were to choose the left fork— although I (certainly but not necessarily) will not. He knows how long it would take me to finish if I were going to make that choice and whether I would encounter a rabbit along the way, and so on.

The question, expressed simply, is this: Does God know counterfactuals? Does he know what would follow from the choices we do not make as well as the things that follow from the choices we do make? Philosophers and theologians, at least some of them, enjoy discussing this question and attempting to argue for one answer or the other.

Obviously, the Bible does not raise this question directly or answer it as such. It is possible, then, that we are left with only logical reasoning as a way of arriving at an answer. Even if we have nothing but human reason to help us, a positive answer is appealing. It seems right to think that God knows what would occur if I did something different from what I actually do. If he knows everything, does he not know what would be different had I gone, say, to a different college or married a different woman? Cannot God directly access the state of being that would follow from decisions we did not make or are not going to make?

Some philosophers are fond of saying that God knows "all possible worlds," and they may affirm that statement as part of this discussion. "All possible worlds" means every conceivable set of circumstances that could ever exist even though only one such "world"—one set of circumstances—actually exists. Perhaps, again, an illustration will help. If I take the right fork tomorrow, various things will follow from that. All those things that occur—a set of circumstances—make up the world that actually is or will be. Should I choose the left fork instead, different things would follow, making a different set of circumstances—a different world—that would actually exist.

Consequently, even though knowing counterfactuals is not quite the same thing as foreknowledge,[11] the two matters become involved together in theological discussion. When applied to foreknowledge, the meaning of knowing counterfactuals boils down to knowing future contingencies. A contingency is an event or situation that could be different from what it

---

[11] As Helm, *Eternal God*, 100, says, "There can only be foreknowledge of things that happen."

is. If a person is really free to choose between two options tomorrow, like whether to have lunch at Wendy's or Cracker Barrel, that choice is a contingency. And if God knows counterfactuals, he knows what will follow from either choice the person makes, both the one he or she will make (factual) and the one he or she will not make (the counterfactual). Again, God knows all possible worlds.

For the purposes of this work, then, this question bears on the discussion of foreknowledge. Fortunately, we are not left with mere logic to arrive at an answer to the question of whether God knows counterfactuals. Although the Bible does not raise or answer the question directly, it does provide an indirect answer by giving us instances of God's knowledge of counterfactuals and of how that works in reference to the future.

One good example is David's experience at Keilah (1 Samuel 23), discussed in chapter 5. In response to David's question, God said that Saul would come there to find him, and that in that case the people of Keilah would betray him to Saul. Both of these were contingencies and were counterfactual. Both were contingent on David's remaining at Keilah—a contingency understood but not expressly stated. David's remaining at Keilah, however, was in a counterfactual world. In the world that actually obtained, David chose to leave and so to avoid the situations that would have occurred, as God knew, had he stayed.

For another example, consider what Jesus said in Matt 11:21: if the works he had done in Chorazin and Bethsaida had been done in Tyre and Sidon, the people in the latter two cities "would have repented in sackcloth and ashes long ago." Likewise, in v. 23, if the works he had done in Capernaum had been done in Sodom, the latter "would have remained until today." In both cases, Jesus claimed to know how things would be different for these cities if they had made a choice other than the one they made. If we take that claim seriously as a claim to real knowledge, which seems unavoidable, it is knowledge of counterfactuals—although in this case it is not foreknowledge.

Yet another example, which does involve knowing the future, clearly presents what will follow from both possible choices when only one will actually be made. This is in Jer 38:17–23, where the prophet confronts King Zedekiah shortly before the fall of Jerusalem to the Babylonians. "If indeed you surrender," Jeremiah says, "this city will not be burned, and you and your household will survive." But "if you do not surrender to the officials of the king of Babylon" (which is what actually transpired) "this city will be handed over to the Chaldeans. They will burn it, and you yourself will not escape from them" (v. 18). Furthermore, in the ensuing conversation Zedekiah excuses himself with the objection that if he should defect, he would fall into the hands of those Jews who had already surrendered and be abused by them. To this Jeremiah offered the clear assurance, "They will not hand you over," that is, into the hands of those Jews. The passage is rife with contingencies, knowledge of counterfactuals, and foreknowledge.

I have no strong desire to make a case for or against God's knowledge of counterfactuals, given that it is a philosophical notion that the Bible does not address except in such examples. It seems important, however, to affirm both that God knows all events in advance and all possibilities, and that his knowledge does not close the door to contingencies that are decided when humans make free (libertarian) choices. This last example is especially powerful in that regard. The options presented to Zedekiah were live options, and what God had in store for him would be different depending on which of the two choices he would make. And I may add that God would have successfully worked his plan either way.

In the end, then, the issue of knowing counterfactuals is not quite the same as foreknowledge, although the two may arise together. Consequently, this issue is not crucial for the basic claims of this book. It will come up again, however, in the discussion of Molinism in the following chapter.

4. The "Simple Foreknowledge" View of Some Arminians

The point of "simple foreknowledge" (SF) is apparently to free God's foreknowledge from other elements, including specifically the knowledge of counterfactuals (as above). However, definitions of SF differ considerably from one writer to another, leaving me uncertain how to respond. I gather that these differences may reflect, at least in part, whether the one defining SF is for it or against it. Open theist Greg Boyd, for example, who is against SF, defines it to mean "that God simply knows what will take place but cannot alter [what will take place] in the light of this knowledge. The fact that God foreknows what will occur does not increase his control over what occurs."[12] Dean Zimmerman, on the other hand, is persuaded that SF allows God some "providential advantages."[13]

David Hunt's definition seems better: "By 'simple' foreknowledge, then, I shall mean the view that the *simple* affirmation [of God's complete and infallible knowledge of the future]—uncomplicated by exceptions, additions, qualifications et cetera—is by itself wholly compatible with human freedom, divine agency and enhanced providential control."[14] By this Hunt means that foreknowledge per se, without being diminished by taking away things like knowledge of future contingencies and without being augmented by things like middle knowledge, is by itself all that is needed to deal with issues like human freedom and divine agency. If everyone would use SF this way, perhaps all who advocate for libertarian freedom could adopt the terminology.

However, there is at least one presentation of SF that is more questionable and needs comment. This is the view of Kevin Jackson, for example, who suggests that God has exhaustive foreknowledge but did not know what choices people would make in this world until (logically) after he had decided to create them.[15] He posits this in reaction to the effort by some

---

[12] Greg A. Boyd, "Problems with Simple Foreknowledge View," ReKnew, February 4, 2015, https://reknew.org/2015/02/problems-with-the-simple-fore knowledge-view/. It seems likely that some Calvinists use "simple foreknowledge" to describe the Arminian view of foreknowledge as not including foreordination.

[13] Dean Zimmerman, "The Providential Usefulness of 'Simple Foreknowledge'," accessed June 21, 2021, http://fas-philosophy.rutgers.edu/zimmerman/Providence .Simple.Forek.6.pdf.

[14] Hunt, "A Simple-Foreknowledge Response," 67.

[15] Kevin Jackson, "An Explanation of Simple Foreknowledge," Society of Evangelical Arminians, April 16, 2012, http://evangelicalarminians.org/an -explanation-of-simple-foreknowledge/.

Calvinists to say that Arminians make God responsible for sin (just as much as they do) since, in the Arminian view, he created the world while fore-knowing the fall and human sin. His idea appears to be that placing God's knowledge of human choices after his decree to create would free God from responsibility for sin.

One wonders if Jackson meant this idea of logical order to be attribut-able to all theologians who hold to SF, but regardless of whether he did, more than one reason exists for rejecting such a presentation of SF. First, the idea misrepresents the omniscience (including foreknowledge) of God. In Jackson's view, one must (at least logically) view God as being ignorant of where his own creative decree would lead. He simply did not know what the free agents he was creating would do. Only after he decreed—and could not take it back—did he learn that Adam, and all his posterity, would sin.

Thus Evan Minton, defending "mere Molinism," quotes Max Andrews's criticism of SF Arminianism as saying that without middle knowledge, before the decree to create, God "did not know what the world would be like. He . . . would not know the actual world until logically-post his creative decree."[16]

Second, Jackson's SF accepts the false argument that for God to create free agents whom he already knew would sin makes God the author of sin. This is not correct. It appears that any Arminians who hold to Jackson's form of SF have made the mistake of allowing the determinists to lead them into that faulty reasoning and so to think they need another construct, dif-ferent from classic Arminianism, to give them a way out. I will address this mistaken idea (which includes a mistaken conception of the nature and implications of foreknowledge) in the next chapter.

Third, the biblical teaching that Jesus was the Lamb of God crucified for our sins before the foundation of the world argues against this version of SF in the same way it argues against open theism (see chap. 9). God had to

---

[16] Max Andrews, "Why I Am Not an Arminian" quoted in Evan Minton, "The Case for Mere Molinism," *Cerebral Faith* (blog), November 7, 2018, https://cerebralfaith.net/the-case-for-mere-molinis/.

know about our sins before creation in order to include his Son's death for us, for sin, in his pre-creation planning.

Regardless, Jackson's view of SF is not the view of God's foreknowledge advocated in this book. Boyd observes that SF is not the position of classic Arminianism; he is right if SF, in general, holds to the view of Jackson. I suspect that most who are classic Arminians would not agree with Jackson on this point.

Conclusion

God's foreknowledge is a wonderful and worshipful ability. In some sense it is a manifestation of God's presence throughout all time. In God's own eternal essence, there is theoretically a body of knowledge that is eternal and unchanging. The way we say this is to describe him as being omniscient. There is no "moment," not logically or temporally, in which he has not known everything knowable.

This knowledge is called foreknowledge when we speak of it in temporal terms, from our perspective in this world of time and space. If it is true, say, that I will visit friends in another state when the coronavirus pandemic has waned, this fact is part of God's knowledge eternally. He knows this today, from within our temporal perspective, and so it is proper (as expressed in chap. 7) to say that he knows it before it happens: thus foreknowledge. I will discuss this again in the following chapter.

Indeed, the following chapter will introduce yet one more issue involved in the important discussion of foreknowledge, bringing discussion of this subject to a close.

ELEVEN

Foreknowledge and Middle Knowledge

D oes God possess middle knowledge? And if he does, what difference does this make for foreknowledge and human freedom? A view known as Molinism—from the name of its founder, Luis de Molina, a sixteenth-century Jesuit priest—answers yes and affirms that this knowledge is key to understanding how God can govern the world in a way that secures both the success of his program and the freedom of human beings to choose. The purpose of this chapter is to analyze Molinism and offer an alternative view built on foreknowledge as presented in the previous chapters.

As was true with the issues treated in the previous chapter, so with the teachings of Molinism: the Bible does not speak directly to these matters. The idea of middle knowledge is a logical construct, and I will explore the implications of this fact later in this chapter. Meanwhile, it is important to explain and evaluate the Molinist viewpoint, given that in recent years it has gained a fairly widespread following. Proponents of Molinism think their view provides a better understanding of the relationship between God's sovereignty and foreknowledge, on the one hand, and our libertarian freedom, on the other.

What Is Molinism?

In short, Molinism says that God has middle knowledge, which means that he knew, before he created us and our world, what any free beings would choose to do in any circumstances possible, including circumstances that never develop.[1] He was able to use this knowledge in designing and actualizing the world and all its circumstances.

Why middle knowledge? There is an old, logical—not temporal—distinction between God's natural or necessary knowledge and his free knowledge. Between these two, Molinists say, is middle knowledge, and the three are logical "moments" in God's knowing, defined as follows.

First, God's natural or necessary knowledge includes everything he knows by virtue of his eternal essence or nature but not what he knows as a result of his decision to bring into existence ("actualize") the created order. Examples include his knowledge of himself as eternal and triune and all self-evident truths like $2 + 2 = 4$. This knowledge also includes all possibilities—"all possible worlds," as philosophers like to say. I will say more about "possible worlds" theory below; for now, a "world" in this phrase is not just the physical cosmos but all the circumstances that exist at any and all times within it—the world and its detailed history, in other words.

Second, God's free knowledge, then, includes everything he knows that logically depends on his decision (decree) to create this world that actually exists—which did not have to exist. God's knowledge of the laws of nature, of the make-up of this universe, of human beings and their actions, is free knowledge and includes his foreknowledge of all that transpires in this world. Theoretically, at least, the contents of this knowledge might have been different from what they are, had he decided to create differently. He

---

[1] When he knows about circumstances that never develop, this brings us back to knowing counterfactuals, as discussed in the previous chapter.

might have decided to locate human beings on a different planet in a different galaxy, for example, or that grass would be orange rather than green, or that John F. Kennedy would not be assassinated.

Third, Molina proposed another "moment" in God's knowledge that stands (logically) between these two: hence middle knowledge. This is knowledge especially related to free beings, and it includes everything such beings would do in all possible sets of circumstances—which involves knowledge of counterfactuals.[2] As a result of knowing this, God decided to create the world and human beings in exactly the circumstances he actualized, being the very circumstances in which would occur the specific free choices that would work for the accomplishing of his will.

The Nature of Molinism

The significant question is whether Molinism is in full accord with the spirit of libertarian freedom or lends itself to a kind of divine control that uses manipulation. In other words, while Molinism deliberately affirms that human choices are freely made, does God indirectly determine these choices by the circumstances he places humans in? I do not intend to paint all Molinists with the brush of determinism; even so, some elements of Molinism raise this question.

There are varieties of Molinism. Some of them lean more toward an Arminian view of God's sovereignty and human freedom, while some seem to be almost as deterministic, in the end, as any form of Calvinism—even if this determinism is indirectly achieved rather than by direct causation.

This much is clear: merely affirming middle knowledge—or the claim that God knew before creation what all conceivable beings would do in all conceivable circumstances—does not make one a Molinist. Molinism depends on how God used that knowledge when he designed and actualized the world. Otherwise, there was no need to propose middle knowledge.

---

[2] These are often called counterfactuals of creaturely freedom (CCFs).

Any view worthy of the name *Molinism*, then, will affirm that God, knowing how free human beings would respond in any circumstances, (1) took that knowledge into account in designing and actualizing the circumstances that exist in the world, and (2) did so as a way to maintain his control and achieve his purpose for the world—without constraining human choices. Perhaps these elements can be interpreted generally enough that individual freedom remains fully intact, or perhaps they can be construed so as to yield "determinism by manipulation," as I would call it.

Regardless, the main claim of Molinism is that the way God maintains control in the world is by knowing how we will respond to various circumstances and then, at the time of creation, tailoring our circumstances accordingly. Molina himself, using some good speech act by Peter as an example, said that this act was "included in the end for which God predetermined to give Peter free choice," explaining that

> God, foreseeing that the act in question would occur by Peter's freedom on the hypothesis that He should will to predetermine all those things, intended *this particular* act and, in accord with His well-pleased will, willed it to exist by means of (i) the predetermination itself, and thus by means of (ii) His providence with respect to that effect, a providence carried out via the predetermination, and, likewise, by means of (iii) the gifts themselves—always with a dependence on Peter's free cooperation, which God foresaw to be forthcoming.[3]

Furthermore, the definitions given to Molinism in the literature, including publications by professed Molinists, confirm this minimum content. Here are some defining examples, which I have chosen from different representations of Molinism.

Eugene Portalié described Molinism thus:

---

[3] Luis de Molina, *On Divine Foreknowledge: Part IV of the Concordia*, trans. Alfred J. Freddoso (Ithaca, NY: Cornell University, 1988), 244. The entire section, 244–53, offers a number of similar explanations.

Before all decision to create the world, the infinite knowledge of God presents to Him all the graces . . . which He can prepare for each soul, along with the consent or refusal which would follow in each circumstance. . . . Thus, for each man in particular there are in the thought of God, limitless possible histories . . . and God will be free in choosing such a world, such a series of graces, and in determining the future history and final destiny of each soul.[4]

Evan Minton, arguing for "Mere Molinism," introduces his discussion with the question, "How Does God Control the Free World?" and illustrates with an example in which God knows that Bob, in circumstance X would freely choose action A and "can decide to create a world in which Bob finds himself in circumstance X and ergo, he chooses action A."[5]

William Lane Craig, arguably evangelicalism's best-known Molinist—and certainly no Calvinist—confirms this understanding:

I'm a libertarian who thinks that causal determinism is incompatible with freedom. That doesn't imply that I hold to the Principle of Alternative Possibilities (PAP), which states that a free agent has in a set of circumstances the ability to choose A or not-A. I'm persuaded that so long as an agent's choice is not causally determined, it doesn't matter if he can actually make a choice contrary to how he does choose. Suppose that God has decided to create you in a set of circumstances because He knew that in those circumstances you would make an undetermined choice to do A. Suppose further that had God instead known that if you were in those circumstances you would have made an undetermined choice to do not-A, then

---

[4] Eugène Portalié, "Teaching of St. Augustine of Hippo," in *The Catholic Encyclopedia*, vol. 2 (New York: Robert Appleton, 1907), as transcribed in Kevin Knight, ed., http://www.newadvent.org/cathen/02091a.htm. I cite this not to vouch for his view that Augustine was thus influenced by what is now known as Molinism, but for its understanding of Molinism. I thank Richard Clark for pointing me to this source.

[5] Minton, "The Case for Mere Molinism" (see chap. 10, n. 16).

God would not have created you in those circumstances (maybe it would have loused up His providential plan!). In that case you do not have the ability in those circumstances to make the choice of not-A, but nevertheless your choice of A is, I think, clearly free, for it is causally unconstrained—it [is] you who determines that A will be done. So the ability to do otherwise is not a necessary condition of free choice.[6]

Craig clearly shows how he understands Molinism to work. God places circumstances in a person's life that he knows will result in the choice that is in accord with God's providential purpose. Furthermore, even for Craig, who professes to believe in libertarian freedom, there is a sense in which this does not really leave the person "free" or able to do otherwise. Thus Craig has dropped one of the key elements in the traditional definition of "libertarian freedom." I would emphasize again that Molinists—including Craig—insist that their view does not entail causal determinism.

Still, some expressions of Molinism appear to me to border on determinism.[7]

---

[6] William Lane Craig, "#23 Middle Knowledge," Reasonable Faith, September 24, 2007, https://www.reasonablefaith.org/writings/question-answer/middle-knowledge.

[7] For a Molinist who affirms unconditional election in a Calvinistic way, see Keathley, *Salvation and Sovereignty* (see chap. 3, n. 18), and see my two-part article: Robert E. Picirilli, "Can Arminians Be Molinists?," Free Will Baptist Theology, September 1, 2020, https://www.fwbtheology.com/can-arminians-be-molinists-part-1/; and September 8, 2020, https://www.fwbtheology.com/can-arminians-be-molinists-part-2/. Keathley does not think the elect "do" anything, not even choose to accept Christ, but that God has placed them in such circumstances of grace that they merely do not resist him and are carried along to saving faith as a gift from God. He does not develop so fully how God's designed circumstances affect the nonelect, but it is clear that God consciously does not put them in circumstances that would lead them to submit to grace. Some Molinists seem to think that the nonelect are those whom God knew would never respond to any gracious circumstances, leaving him helpless to draw them to himself, but Matt 11:21 makes clear that God knew circumstances that would have brought to repentance some who

Why Reject Molinism?

First, the key here is that before he willed our existence, God willed the circumstances of human existence in accord with his knowledge of how each individual would respond to those circumstances. This is the way God exercises his providential control over the world. Indirectly, then, this understanding at least opens the door to say that he determined our responses. The traditional libertarian does not believe that this is the way God exercises his providential government of the world and secures its success. Instead, he is in full control regardless of what choices we make. By means of his foreknowledge, God's plan incorporates all our choices, but it does not "set the table" for those choices.

Second, in the lengthy quotation from Craig above, one notices that he has given up the power of alternative (or contrary) choice as being required for libertarian freedom. Craig insists that he maintains libertarian freedom, but for those who, like me, regard libertarian freedom, by definition, as including the power of alternative or contrary choice, that seems questionable. When he says that all that is required for libertarian freedom is that a person's choice not be causally constrained, a compatibilist could say the very same thing, even if with a different end in view.

Third, Molinism, with its distinctions between the three "moments" of God's knowledge, is a philosophical-logical construct—an abstraction—that does not provide an understanding as to how God's all-inclusive, providential government of the world can be harmonized with human freedom. As David Basinger observed, Molinists cannot avoid having God decide which sets of circumstances—and therefore which human responses—to actualize.[8] (More about logical constructs below.)

---

never repented. I contend that God's reason for not placing them in different circumstances was something other than his knowledge of how they would or would not respond.

[8] David Basinger, "Divine Control and Human Freedom: Is Middle Knowledge the Answer?," *Journal of the Evangelical Theological Society* 36, no. 1 (1993): 55–64.

Fourth, applying Molinism to specific instances of the exercise of moral agency, especially to instances when a person chooses against God's will, proves difficult and telling. For Molinists, tailoring the world's circumstances to the responses God knows people will make is his way of maintaining his providential government. In that case, this method must be applied to all choices, whether for good or evil. As examples, consider biblical narratives regarding Judas and Adam and Eve.

When we say God knew in advance how Judas would respond to any conceivable circumstances, that would mean, say, that (1) he knew just how Judas would respond to the circumstances that actually were in place; and (2) he knew how Judas would respond if the circumstances were different in some way—say, his friends advised him against betraying Jesus, or the priests only offered fifteen pieces of silver. Molinism cannot avoid saying that God deliberately chose, as part of this world he actualized, the very circumstances in which he knew that Judas would betray Jesus—and for that very reason. Molina regarded evil acts as permitted by God, but even those he said "are subject as well to divine predetermination and providence . . . for the sake of some greater good."[9] Alfred Freddoso, Molina's translator and interpreter, applies this to Peter's denial of Jesus: "Given that God knows infallibly by His middle knowledge that Peter would in fact freely deny Christ if placed in those circumstances, it follows that by decreeing that Peter will be in those circumstances God ensures that it is true from eternity that Peter will freely sin."[10]

To be fair, Molinism insists that Judas's decision was still free and unforced, but the point of Molinism is that God chose Judas's circumstances, though not directly to cause him to betray Jesus, but for the very purpose of providing the circumstances in which he knew Judas would do so. In the case of Adam and Eve, the same considerations apply.

There is a fine but important distinction here. For the traditional libertarian, God's exhaustive foreknowledge means that he knew when he

---

[9] Molina, *Divine Foreknowledge*, 252.
[10] Molina, 54.

created Adam and Eve (and Judas), in the circumstances he placed them in, that they would fail him. Is this ultimately the same thing as Molinism? No, and the difference is that God did not provide that set of circumstances because he knew they would sin if he did. Instead, God placed them in that set of circumstances in spite of knowing that they would sin and for an entirely different reason: to provide the testing he deemed necessary.

In other words, Adam and Eve did not have to sin, and God did not desire that they sin, nor did he place them in their circumstances with a purpose of indirectly bringing about their sin. Obviously, he wanted them to be free to sin, and for reasons best known to him, they needed to be tested. Their circumstances contributed to nothing more than their being tempted; their failure was their own doing, and their circumstances were not constructed so as to enable God to achieve his will by their sin. He achieved his will by their testing, by their making a free choice as he had designed them to make, and by how he dealt with them in response to their sin, including his provision of grace. Surely his will would have been achieved—perhaps even more fully and more immediately—had they resisted the temptation as he desired.

A merely human illustration may help. I may know someone—my wife, say—well enough to be confident as to how she will respond if I put her in a certain situation. I may then indeed put her in that situation. The question is why I do so. I may do it in order to elicit that response from her, which would be manipulative. Or I may do it because it is the right thing for me to do regardless of how she is expected to respond. That would not be manipulative. The difference is that in the first I would be constructing the circumstances to produce the response, while in the latter I would not take her anticipated response into consideration when deciding to construct the circumstances for other reasons. Molinism says that God constructs human circumstances in the way that accords with the response he knows they will make, and that he does this as his way of maintaining his providential government of all things.

This is the difference between traditional libertarian freedom and Molinism. As represented in this book, God conceived and created this world to be the arena in which he acts and interacts with human beings in an interpersonal way, providing circumstances that are both friendly to their freedom and designed to test them and provide opportunity for them to submit to God freely. He does not create them in a way that designs in advance the circumstances in which he knows they will respond to his overtures. God maintains control regardless of how human beings respond in their choices. Where real choices are present, God's control is not at stake. Had Abraham obeyed or disobeyed when he was tested, God's plan would not have been thwarted. In order to maintain providential government of the world, he does not need any individual to make a particular one of the open choices. God will succeed whether we submit to him or rebel.

Here is one more illustration, this one biblical and involving Jeroboam. Even before Jeroboam became king over the breakaway northern tribes, Yahweh spoke to him through a prophet (1 Kgs 11:26–40), telling him what was going to come about. Among the things Yahweh said was the wonderful promise of v. 38 (NKJV): "If you heed all that I command you, walk in My ways, and do *what is* right in My sight, to keep My statutes and My commandments . . . I will be with you and build for you an enduring house, as I built for David, and will give Israel to you" (emphasis added).

We are woefully familiar with what transpired instead. Jeroboam, acting in deliberate self-will, instituted a false religion for Israel (12:25–33). He made a rival altar to substitute for the place of sacrifice in Jerusalem, cast two golden bull calves as rival gods to be in Dan and Bethel, and consecrated a rival priesthood—all this of his own invention (v. 26: "said to himself"). When he was challenged by a man of God, his arm and hand were paralyzed, and he was reduced to begging the man to pray for his healing, a prayer that was answered (13:1–6). And yet for all that the final word was, "Jeroboam did not repent of his evil way" (v. 33). And his sin became the cause of Israel's stumbling into idolatry (v. 34). The words of 14:16 are full of pathos: "He [Yahweh] will give up Israel because of Jeroboam's sins that he committed and caused Israel to commit."

God set before Jeroboam two paths, and Jeroboam chose the wrong one when he could have chosen the right one, enabled by the word and

Spirit of God. The success of God's plan, of his government of the world, did not depend on his making either choice. In his foreknowledge, God knew the choice Jeroboam would make and incorporated that into his plan. God would have remained in sovereign control either way; he is all able. In Molinism, however, the success of God's plan depends on his providing for certain choices by fixing the circumstances in which those choices occur. A more robust view of libertarian freedom and God's ability does not need that.

The Problem of Logical Constructs

The idea that God's knowledge can be better understood in terms of "moments," with "middle knowledge" standing between natural or necessary knowledge and free knowledge, is a man-made, logical-philosophical-theological construct (hereafter "construct"). As indicated in the preface, I am not inveighing against such constructs, since some are very important and helpful; even so, all constructs must be understood for what they are and used carefully.

The best constructs—like the Trinity or the theanthropic person of Christ—have won the long-standing approval of the Christian church in general and can be used without hesitation. One keeps in mind, however, that even the good constructs (1) represent the best we can do in our human reasoning, and (2) represent important truths even if in some ways they express those truths both equivocally and univocally.

For constructs that have not won wide approval in the church, we should keep yet one more thing in mind: that philosophers or theologians develop such constructs as a means of expressing a concept in a logical and orderly way. The theologian needs to ask, What is a given construct meant to say? How do we express, in more ordinary language, the truths that any construct appears to support but only represents?

No human being can possibly know how God's knowledge occurs to him, and the Bible does not give this information; I'm confident Molinists will agree. So what is this construct—that God experiences knowledge in (logical) "moments"—meant to say? Perhaps it represents the truth—an obvious one—that there is order and relationship within a body of knowledge. Some things known are basic "first" truths, while others follow logically from or build on them—at least in our knowing. In God's eternal knowledge—his omniscience, that is—there is certainly no temporal movement of ideas or "learning" of anything by reasoning from one thing to another. (See some observations in this regard in chap. 2 on immutability.)

Middle knowledge was likewise conceived to provide a logical framework within which to express and understand a concept. That concept, apparently, is that God must logically first know things possible, then things that would be if any of those possible things actually existed, and then what will be, following from his decision to actualize one of those possibilities. Middle knowledge amounts to nothing more than that, and the affirmation of it merely represents the affirmer's view that this must be so. Yet Molinism's development of the idea and use of middle knowledge is intended to say that the way God controls things (in his exhaustive providence) in this world is by knowing how people will respond to various circumstances and arranging, even before their existence, the circumstances in which they will respond in accord with the plan he intends by his government.

Such a construct, therefore, cannot be used as an argument in support of the concept it was constructed to express. The concept of middle knowledge expresses a theory of how God experienced his knowledge and how he used it in designing the created order; it cannot then be an argument for that theory. As a construct, it represents the view, but it does not argue for the view. If one uses it as an argument, one is arguing in a circle—not to mention begging the question of whether God has middle knowledge or uses it as Molinists claim.

Here is an example of a circular argument, wrongly used by a Molinist against the view called "simple foreknowledge"—which is also a construct, discussed in the previous chapter. Mere Molinist Evan Minton rejects "simple foreknowledge Arminianism" and offers two quotations as arguments against it.[11] The first quotation is from Max Andrews in "Why I'm Not an

---

[11] Minton, "The Case for Mere Molinism."

Arminian": "If God has merely two logical moments of knowledge (natural and free) then logically prior to God's decree of creation he did not know what the world would be like. He could know all possible worlds prior to the decree but he would not know the actual world until logically-post [after] his creative decree."[12]

The flaw in this is easy to spot. Andrews has assumed the position being argued for and used it as an argument for the position. He believes in a middle moment as he and other Molinists have defined it and the first and third moments around it. Andrews, in effect, is arguing thus: "I believe in three moments and in what each can include, so the simple foreknowledge view must be wrong." That is not a cogent argument; it is subtly restating his position as though it were an argument. One might simply counter it, for example, by affirming that God's necessary knowledge included what agents would do in circumstances in the world.

Minton's other quotation is from William Lane Craig: "[The view that there is no middle knowledge means that] God, logically before the divine decree [to create, has] . . . no knowledge of what would happen under any circumstances. Thus, logically posterior to the divine decree, God must consider himself extraordinarily lucky to find that this world happened to exist."[13] The quotation goes on to say that in that case God did not even know, posterior to the divine decree, whether Herod or Pilate or the Israelite nation would exist.

Craig's argument has the very same problem as that of Andrews. He believes in middle knowledge, of course, and he defines it as including what God knew would happen under all circumstances. Growing out of that he says that without middle knowledge God could not know what would happen under any circumstances in this world when he decided to create it.

---

[12] Andrews, "Why I Am Not an Arminian," quoted in Minton.

[13] William Lane Craig, "'No Other Name': A Middle Knowledge Perspective on the Exclusivity of Salvation through Christ," Reasonable Faith, accessed July 6, 2021, https://www.reasonablefaith.org/writings/scholarly-writings/christian-particularism /no-other-name-a-middle-knowledge-perspective-on-the-exclusivity-of-salvatio/, quoted in Minton.

His argument amounts to saying that since middle knowledge by definition includes everything that would happen under all circumstances, a creator without it could not know what creatures will do until after his decision to create them. That argument assumes his own distinction between middle and necessary knowledge and then uses it as an argument for middle knowledge. Anyone who provides, in his system, a way for God to know every "would" in human choices can simply deny that Craig's system is true or his argument convincing. Surely we can account for God's foreknowledge in a different way, including the alternative outlined below.

The Possibility of Logical Issues within Molinism

Before offering an alternative, however, some brief suggestions as to whether Molinism is logically coherent are in order. Molinism offers what appear to be some inconsistencies.

First, mainly, Molinism appears illogical in its implication that God does not know what free agents would do in all conceivable circumstances as part of his knowledge of all possible worlds; this leads Molinists to a separate (middle) "moment." Although I am not fond of "possible worlds" theory, to argue this point I must couch my observations in the terminology of that framework.

Molinism says that God knows, as part of his natural or necessary knowledge, "all possible worlds." Now, the difference between possible worlds involves what free agents can decide in various circumstances. Perhaps the best way to communicate this is to use a specific illustration, one that works in the same way for every free choice. Consider Abraham's testing in the matter of God's command to sacrifice Isaac. In one "world" Abraham obeys; in another "world" he disobeys. Molinists affirm that God knows both of those worlds, among possible worlds, in the first moment of his knowledge.

The point, then, is this: if he already knows both of those worlds exhaustively, even though only as possibilities ("could be"), then he already knows everything that will be if he should decide to actualize either of those worlds. He logically does not need to know something else between these two moments.

Anyone pursuing this needs to think carefully and deeply about what it really means for God to know fully any possible world. In his natural knowledge, God already knows the full history of every world he conceives. All "worlds" he "knows" are worlds he conceives.

Second, another logical problem arises when we consider that most of people's alternative choices, the moral ones at any rate, come in the same set of circumstances. This does not fit in well with "possible worlds" theory, for one thing, or with God's anticipating how people will respond to various circumstances and tailoring their circumstances accordingly. Using again the illustration of Abraham, the point is that he could have chosen to obey or disobey without the circumstances being any different. That is an essential part of what it means to have libertarian freedom. If nothing else, this possibility shows that the idea of God's using circumstances as a means of securing the human responses he intends is questionable if not illogical, given that Abraham could obey or disobey in the very same circumstances.

A response to this may take the form of observing that if Abraham can obey or disobey under exactly the same circumstances, choices are random, unpredictable, unknowable acts, and in that case the only way for God to maintain control would be by predetermining all choices. The course to steer between determinism and randomness, however, is the course of self-determination, sometimes spoken of as agent causality. Human beings, bearing (or being) the image of God, cause or determine their own actions and can choose to obey or disobey from within themselves without any circumstances being different.[14] This understands human action (and human–divine interaction) not as expressing a cause-and-effect relationship but an influence-response relationship. Humans make decisions and initiate events in consideration of whatever reasons they wish to consider.[15]

---

[14] I have written elsewhere in this volume about the fact that God can foreknow such self-determined choices, including that we are not required to explain how he can know them.

[15] Thus, free human choices are explainable, and if they are explainable, they are knowable. I am not attempting, however, to explain how God can foreknow free choices; as I have said elsewhere, I feel no need to explain how God knows anything.

Third, another objection to what I have said will take the form of insisting that it is logically necessary for God—as for any of us—to know first what can or could be, then what people would do in any conceivable circumstance, and, only when he chooses and actualizes a particular world, what they will do in it. I would ask why God must "know" in this way. It seems clear that God's knowing what is possible logically entails his knowing what will be if he decides to actualize the possible. In other words, there is but one logical step needed to move from the conception of possibilities to their actual existence: the decision to actualize a world already known as possible.

Fourth, another logical flaw may exist in the same relationship: that if God already knows all the details of any possible world in his natural knowledge, he has no further opportunity to tinker with that world in choosing circumstances in accord with knowing how people will respond. In other words, if he knows everything in that possible world, he already knows all the circumstances therein, which he himself conceived. And if he conceived them before he knew how people would respond, as Molinists say, then he could not change the circumstances before actualizing the world. On the other hand, if, as suggested above, God designed the "circumstances" of this world for reasons other than to ensure certain responses from free agents, and in spite of knowing how they would respond, there is no need for adjusting circumstances after gaining more knowledge at a logical middle moment.

Anyone evaluating Molinism should rigorously examine its logic. Even so, the possibility of logical lapses in Molinism is not the most important criticism of it. That criticism is its claim that the way God providentially governs the world is by knowing the choices people will make in advance and building into creation the circumstances that will lead to the choices his plan requires.

Alfred Freddoso may be right in saying that if there will be adequate grounds for the truth of a future fact at that time, then there is now adequate metaphysical grounds for the truth of it. Molina, *Divine Foreknowledge*, 72. Freddoso's discussion in "Knowledge of Conditional Future Contingents" (78–81) is at least very interesting.

A Foreknowledge Alternative to Middle Knowledge

The main lines of an alternative to Molinism seem fairly obvious in the previous discussion. This more traditional, and more plausible, view does not rest on a concept called "simple foreknowledge," if this means that God did not possess foreknowledge of free choices until (logically) after his decree to create free agents. In this alternative view "foreknowledge" needs no modifiers; it is the foreknowledge defined and defended in the previous chapters. This foreknowledge is intuitive and exhaustive; God eternally enjoys immediate and direct access to all of history.

First, whether there were any other possible worlds, the world God created (actualized) is a world he conceived.[16] Creation, after all, is ex nihilo. Even the so-called necessary truths, like 2 + 2 = 4, are truths that in some way are grounded in God's own eternal existence and consciousness—his nature or being, in other words. No world is "possible" except as God makes it so.[17]

Second, and furthermore, reverting to "possible worlds" terminology for a moment, the main thing that makes for different possibilities, at least in this world, is the freedom of human agents to choose between alternatives. Consider again the example of Abraham's testing. Rather than say there were two "possible worlds" in that incident, I find it much more preferable to say that God created a world in which Abraham could obey or disobey.

Out of all possibilities, then, God conceived the world he intended to create. As discussed in chapter 3, he conceived this world eternally. He knew it perfectly, even while it was yet only a conceptual possibility, and that means he knew all its history from beginning to end.

---

[16] There is or was no preexisting number of possible worlds somewhere in the realm of "necessary" truths, no Platonic universals or forms that God could contemplate, for example.

[17] Any world God conceived as possible was, ipso facto, a world he could actualize. I see little or no benefit in distinguishing between feasible worlds (which he could actualize) and worlds only logically possible but unfeasible, at least not for the discussion here.

Third, it follows necessarily that God, at the (eternal) "moment" of conceiving our discrete world (among any other possibilities he conceived, if there were any), knew exactly what any of the persons he conceived in this world would do in all its circumstances (which he conceived as part of this world) if he should choose to actualize it. I contend that if he knew any less than that, he did not fully know the "world" being spoken of or its possibilities.[18]

Fourth, this entails, then, that in knowing this world perfectly, he not only knew that Abraham really could obey or disobey, he knew which choice Abraham actually would make and all that would follow from that choice. If that were not the case, he would not have known this world completely. And he knew this necessarily and eternally.

Again, God conceived this world, with all the actors and all the circumstances in which they act. Those circumstances included the initial circumstances that existed at the "moment" of creation: Adam and Eve in Eden, soon to be approached by Satan, and so on. And the world he conceived included all the circumstances that would follow, depending on which choice Adam and Eve made and all the choices to be made by all the free agents thereafter.

Fifth, it follows that in conceiving and fully knowing this world, even when it was only a possibility, God knew from the first, eternal "moment" of his knowledge—in his omniscience, that is—everything needed to create a world he would exhaustively and immediately foreknow. Indeed, by virtue of conceiving this world, with its agents and circumstances, and the choices they would freely make, he knew everything that would transpire if he should actualize it. Then at the moment he decided to actualize this world, God already possessed eternal, intuitive foreknowledge of everything in this world.

---

[18] That he also knew this about any other world he conceived is relatively unimportant for our theology and understanding of the Bible. It is also relatively unimportant whether this world is the best of all possible worlds, which is a key issue involved in "possible worlds" theory.

Sixth, this foreknowledge of God's, then, did not have to "wait" for the decision to create; from knowing everything about this world as a possibility he conceived he already knew everything about it as a world he would create. Foreknowledge precedes creation, and the Bible's references to Jesus as the Lamb slain "before the foundation of the world" make this clear (see the earlier discussion of this). Beginning with the moment of the world's creation, God's knowledge of events in this world can be called foreknowledge since it has the context of this temporal world and is spoken from our perspective. (See comments on this in chap. 7.)

Seventh, a final element of this alternative to Molinism deals with God's arrangement of circumstances when conceiving and actualizing this world. As noted, his eternal conception of this world, as the one he would actualize, already included all the free agents and their circumstances and choices. Whether he considered alternate "possible worlds" in conceiving and actualizing this one, then, is speculative and not essential to my view. Once he conceived this world he would actualize, it was "too late" in his knowing, then, to arrange circumstances conducive to the agents' making choices that God intended as ends of his providential government.

To say this another way, God did not, in advance of creating, arrange circumstances in accord with his knowledge of how free agents would respond to them. Instead, the world he conceived and actualized was by design friendly to free agency. The circumstances he conceived for this world were chosen for reasons more basic than how people would respond to them. He loved both those who would submit to his wooing and those who would not. He placed all of them in gracious circumstances without regard to how they would choose. He made equal provision for their salvation and drew them all, in his prevenient, enabling grace, to himself, both those who would yield and those who would resist. His salvific intention was manifested to them all, and he labored with them all to bring them to himself, genuinely desiring that they all be saved. Middle knowledge is not needed for this view of how he brings people to himself.

This alternative to Molinism is also a construct since the Bible itself does not discuss such matters. But, instead of two or three "moments" of knowledge, it has just one: God's eternal omniscience in which he conceived this world as it is—among all possibilities, if there were any others. The only other "moment" is the moment of creation. He knew forever what "world" he would create. (See again the discussion in chap. 3 regarding his eternal purpose to create the world that he actualized at the beginning of time.)

Does This Alternative Make God the Cause of All Things, Including Sin?

Perhaps the major objection to what I have proposed is that it appears to make God the cause of every event in this world and author of sin. That objection goes something like this: if God knew before he created this world everything that everyone would do in it, and with his "Let there be" actualized this world in which all events were certain, then he must be the one who actualized—and so caused—every so-called free choice including the sins that agents commit. That thinking makes God responsible.

This conclusion is apparently the reason some Arminians invented the approach of "simple foreknowledge"—instead of traditional, eternal, exhaustive, intuitive foreknowledge—as discussed in the previous chapter. It is also the reason for the invention of open theism by neo-Arminians, which denies that God foreknew our sins, as discussed in chapter 9.

This objection is entirely unwarranted, and the issue is relatively simple. That God created people who sinned, exercising the freedom he gave them, does not make him morally responsible for their sin—not unless he placed them in circumstances where they had to sin or directly caused them to sin. In the world God actualized he placed free, self-determined agents who could obey or disobey him, and implicit in that possibility is his permission for sin to exist. The free agents he created brought sin into the world. God is not the author of sin; he is the author of freedom.

The fact that God created this very world in which Adam and all his posterity were certain to sin, and God knew it, does not make him the cause of their free choices or their sin. To be sure, there are all sorts of word games that people play, and no doubt some can define "responsible" and "cause" in a way that enables them to say that God is the cause of everything and is responsible for sin.

Yes, God is responsible for creating this world in which he knew there would be much sin and evil. Every theologian must come to grips with that fact. God is responsible for the possibility of sin as a result of creating beings who can sin. When God created people as moral, causal agents, he opened the door to sin and evil. But sin and evil are not "necessities" in any sense of that word.

Obviously, to create a world where human beings have the freedom to choose for or against God was important to him. That was his will. And in his sovereignty, he was free to create the world of his choice—out of all possibilities. He chose freedom; he chose people who could voluntarily give him their love or withhold it. He desires that everyone love him and goes to unimaginable lengths to draw all to himself in grace (John 12:32). Beyond all doubt, he has "no pleasure in the death of the wicked" (Ezek 33:11). Even so, he gave us the power—and thereby the permission—to sin. It was his active will to provide for that possibility.

Naturally, we feel compelled to ask why. Why would God create a world where he knew sin and evil would arise? I confess that I do not know the answer, that no answer that has been proposed seems fully satisfactory. Even so, I am certain that there is an answer, that God knows it very well, and that it is absolutely just. Meanwhile, my not knowing why sin exists does not make God responsible for it. He has revealed where the responsibility lies. He did not want anyone to sin; he did not "need" sin.

Someone may ask, But could not he have created a world where there would be no sin and evil? Maybe, maybe not. It is not in our power to know the answer to this question. Perhaps a world of free, moral agents without sin and evil was not possible. But we do not know that; no one can know that now. If there really were possible worlds, other than this one, he could have chosen to actualize, that possibility remains known to him alone. Whatever the case, God is not glad for sin or for anyone's eternal separation from him. He made no one for that direct purpose, even though he made some persons as "vessels" (NKJV) he knew would be objects of his eternal wrath (Rom 9:22)—and did everything he could, within the parameters of the world, as he designed and created it, to keep them from remaining under his wrath. I cannot imagine that he is better glorified as a result of there being sin in the world, but I am aware that what I cannot imagine is puny and impotent.

The Fallacy of Arguments from Foreknowledge

Because this is my final chapter about foreknowledge, I close with a discussion about the way some theologians misuse God's foreknowledge. God's foreknowledge does not produce reality, and it does not change the relations between things.

With respect to the matter just discussed, consider this question: Does the fact that God created people who could sin make him responsible for their sin? Whether one answers yes or no, the point here is that adding foreknowledge into that picture changes nothing about the relationship and offers no reason for one answer or the other. One may argue that God's creating people capable of sin makes or does not make him responsible for their sin, but adding that he knew what they would do when he created them neither weakens nor strengthens either answer.

The problem is that people, theologians included, get it in their heads that foreknowledge of an event makes that event reality. People cannot quite seem to help themselves in taking something talked about as foreknown as though it is already reality. Such a conclusion is not true. I cannot overestimate the importance of correcting this misunderstanding of foreknowledge and putting it in the right perspective. Nearly all arguments based on foreknowledge assume that foreknowledge makes real what is foreknown and are therefore fallacious.

As chapter 7 made clear, the idea that foreknowledge is reality is mistaken. But theologians, including some logicians who ought to know better, persist in thinking that God's foreknowledge settles things. They are mistaken; something foreknown in the future is not already reality.

An illustration may help. Sometimes people say that once a person receives Christ as Savior, God forgives all of that person's sins, past, present, and future. They seem to think that if God knows a person's future sins, he must forgive them now or else the person is not in right relationship with him. (And, of course, they appropriately want the person to have assurance of salvation.)

But a future sin, even one known by God, is not yet a sin. A person is not now guilty of a sin that has not yet been committed; therefore, that person does not now need forgiveness. We simply have to decide—it is an act of the will—to stop viewing foreknowledge this way. God knows the person has not committed that sin. He knows the person does not have to sin. He knows it is really possible for the person not to commit the sin, as 1 Cor 10:13 indicates. To be sure, whatever God knows a person is going to do will occur, but his foreknowledge of that in no way settles, or necessitates, or influences, or even makes certain anything done freely in the future.

The same fallacious thinking is involved when anyone argues that it is incoherent for God to make persuasive efforts toward people whom he foreknows will not respond. But people can only "not respond" when they have been wooed; they do not "not respond" until efforts have been made toward them. Foreknowledge of a person's response does not make the response reality. A response foreknown is not yet a response.

This is similar to the argument that if God knows the future we cannot do anything to change it. The future does not become reality until we have done whatever it is we are going to do, and not even God's knowledge of that future makes it reality before then. We have not done it yet. We do not have to do it. Even when God knows we will do it, he also knows we really can do otherwise. Until we start thinking this way, we will continue fallacious reasoning about foreknowledge.

To illustrate, let us say that a friend has just invited me to lunch. I do not have any conflicting activity going on, so I can accept or decline. I choose to accept. Now, God in foreknowledge knew all this yesterday (or at any other time in the past). But God's foreknowledge made absolutely no contribution to bringing this about. It was not reality until it occurred. The invitation was not extended until my friend contacted me. The choice to accept was not made until I decided. If I had decided to decline the invitation, God's foreknowledge would have accorded with that; in that case he would never—could never—have known that I would accept.

Foreknowledge is not in itself a force; it does not "settle" anything. Foreknowledge does not cause anything. Foreknowledge does not "render certain" anything. Even God's creating this world while knowing every free choice people will make did not "make certain" any of their moral choices. The future is certain to God, but he did not make certain any of its contingencies that depend on human free choices.

Arguments regarding certainty have been made in previous chapters; if those arguments are sound, the future fact, which God knows as a certainty, is not yet a reality. Its certainty is grounded in the fact itself, not in God's knowing the fact. Neither God's knowing now what someone will do, nor his knowing when he created the world, renders any contingent event certain. Only an agent's choice renders certain that choice. One must be able to see that God can know now a future fact that will not be made certain until it is a fact in actual history. That is what foreknowledge of the future means, and this is the view of foreknowledge maintained throughout this book.

Conclusion

No doubt God had an ultimate and all-inclusive plan in mind when he created the universe and human beings. And no doubt he knew, when he did so, that his plan would be effectively achieved. But that overall achievement does not eliminate the give-and-take of divine–human interaction—influence and response, in other words—in the course of history he set in motion when he actualized the world we are part of, knowing everything that would follow.

Such exhaustive, intuitive foreknowledge does not need middle knowledge, although we can appreciate the fact that some Molinists make a deliberate effort to preserve human freedom. It is apparently true that God knows how each human being would decide and act in any given set of circumstances—which is to say that he knows counterfactuals or "all possible worlds."

No doubt God's knowing how people will respond in any set of circumstances is useful to him in providentially governing human affairs in this world without constraining their wills. I have often said, for example, that I may plan to go work in my garden tomorrow, and God can stop me if he needs to, without constraining my will, by sending rain. Furthermore, there are times when God has finished offering grace and proceeds to the exercise of judgment. In the case of the Egyptian pharaoh in Moses's day, for example, God might well have chosen to act in ways that he knew Pharaoh would resist and that would harden his heart. (See the subsequent chapter on the exodus.) Second Thessalonians 2:11 is a case in point.

Molinism, however, says much more about God's providential government: that before we existed, God, knowing how we would respond to every possible circumstance, arranged our circumstances in accord with that knowledge and in accord with his will for us. Whenever that kind of thinking results in arranging things advantageously for some and not for others, this appears to be manipulative, and the word *freedom* is so qualified that it is suspect. Determinists also insist that they are defending freedom—as they define the word.

My reference to the difference between what God is doing in this world and before we existed intentionally reflects the major theme of this book. Like determinists, Molinists tend to focus on what God knew and decided and did in his eternal existence and then to allow that focus to dominate their view of what happens in time and space. Instead, we ought to focus primarily on what God does in time and space, as revealed in the Bible, and allow that vision to provide an understanding of what he has done in eternity. What God is really about is shown in his interaction with human beings in this world, and that is when he uses his perfect knowledge of the very hearts and tendencies of people to exercise his providential arrangement of circumstances on behalf of his will for them, as indicated in Rom 8:28. The intersection between time and eternity, referred to in chapter 8, means that what God does in time is revelatory of his knowledge and acts in eternity. The one does not determine the other; they are both the same.

More important, middle knowledge has little if anything to contribute to answering the question of how human freedom is reconciled with God's sovereignty and foreknowledge. It is far better to "solve" the apparent problem between God's exhaustive foreknowledge and human freedom in the way set forth in chapter 7 and in the alternative proposed above. Yes, when he created human beings and the world of time and space God knew everything that would follow. But he did not settle all the details and choices by the circumstances he put in motion.[19] Instead, he allowed human beings, as he designed them, to make real choices in situations in which they had the ability to choose otherwise; that is, they could exercise libertarian freedom. For Molinism, God maintains control by ordaining the circumstances that will produce the choices or responses that enable the achievement of his purpose. For traditional libertarians, God maintains control and achieves his plan regardless of which of two (or more) alternative choices free agents will make.

Better still, because he loved all human beings, he dealt with all in accord with the same sincere salvific motivations, to provide for and draw them to himself. His prevenient grace was extended to all and enabled all who hear the gospel under the influence of the Holy Spirit to accept what he had provided and was "drawing" them to. Foreknowing how it would work out exhaustively, he provided for true influence-and-response interaction between himself and human beings. At the same time, he was able to work in all situations, regardless of which moral choices they would make along the way. He knew but did not predetermine their decisions, not even by the circumstances he placed them in.

To be sure, even this account means that whatever human beings decide, God's "will"—in an important sense—is accomplished. This concept is not hard to grasp. If, for example, he designs human beings with the freedom

---

[19] It is true that when God actualized us and our world, knowing exactly what we would do, the course of history was certain to him, but since he ordained a world in which we have libertarian freedom, he did not put us in circumstances in which our choices were necessary, which is the sense in which I use "settled." (As I have indicated previously, perhaps the Thomist distinction between absolute and relative or suppositional necessity is involved.)

to choose for or against him, making such a choice is his will for them constitutionally. Whatever their choice, they are fulfilling this design—God's will—in determining their own destiny. By its very nature, this will of design takes precedence over, is more fundamental than, the will of his desire that all of those whom he designed to choose for themselves would choose him and be saved. Theologians of all stripes have always found it necessary to make some distinctions between aspects of God's will, and this distinction seems helpful. It is no contradiction to affirm that God, on the one hand, wills for us to choose and so for those who choose against him to be eternally separated from him, and that he, on the other hand, wills that all be saved.[20]

How, then, should we understand foreknowledge? It does not mean that things are settled and our choices meaningless. They are as unsettled and meaningful as our experience tells us they are, as they would be even if God did not know them. Foreknowledge means, however, that God is also involved with us, that he is aware of our lives and decisions, that he has included us and our circumstances in his plans, that he provides for us, protects and guides us in full knowledge of every situation we will face, and will do everything commensurate with his will for the way the world operates—everything in his power, in other words—to ensure that we make the right decisions. But he created us, designed us, to make those decisions, and his foreknowledge, as reassuring as it is, does not relieve us of the responsibility or of the consequences.

---

[20] Many theologians distinguish between such aspects of God's will as his "antecedent" and "consequent" wills. I have no objection to this terminology but prefer "design" and "desire."

PART THREE

Wrapping Up

TWELVE

God and Man and Theology in the Exodus

Up to now, a number of biblical examples have illustrated the inter-action between God and human beings. The Exodus account offers many more illustrations of God and humans acting back and forth in time and space in influence-and-response mode. This chapter will explore this highly interesting drama. There is much to be learned here, underscoring the perspective developed in this work.

Even a theologically liberal interpreter recognizes that a narrative like Exodus intentionally represents God as working in history.

> "God is known by what He has done." This sentence sums up one of the leading themes of biblical theology. The biblical writers (it is said) thought of revelation, not in terms of propositions or ideas, but as taking place through historical events in which God disclosed

His nature and purpose. Moreover, these events were not the inner spiritual experiences of mystics, but public events.[1]

Tomes concludes that "the assertion that God has acted in history has no value unless it is a judgment on actual and not idealised history."[2]

I have no desire to get involved in scholarly debates about external issues such as the date of the exodus. On such matters, it is enough to say that I regard the account as historically grounded and accurate. There is no good reason to abandon the traditional view of an early date—say, 1445 BC—or to think that the original author of the work as a whole, inspired by God, was anyone other than the Moses who led Israel out of bondage in Egypt.

The Initiating Circumstance

As often noticed, Genesis closed with Joseph "in a coffin in Egypt" (Gen 50:26). Exodus—a name literally meaning the "way out" or "departure"—opens where Genesis left off and moves quickly across the 400 years or so that followed the relocation of the old man Israel and his large brood to Egypt. The narrative wastes no time on details, summarizing to inform us that the young nation had come to experience bitter enslavement. Except for a subtle reminder or two, God seems absent as the account gets underway, as noted by Roger Owens.[3] Two short chapters take us right to the circumstance in which God began to act.[4]

---

[1] Roger Tomes, "Exodus 14: The Mighty Acts of God: An Essay in Theological Criticism," *Scottish Journal of Theology* 22, no. 4 (December 1969): 455.

[2] Tomes, 478.

[3] Owens, "Free, Present, and Faithful," 614–27 (see chap. 1, n. 15). He suggests, appropriately enough, that this absence raises a question about the character of God, "and the narrative, as it proceeds, will draw the portrait of God" (619–20).

[4] Already the hand of God has been noted, in passing, in his blessing of the Hebrew midwives who feared him (Exod 1:20–21). I will not undertake to comment on every single mention of God's work in the record.

That circumstance gets a sharp, no-nonsense definition in 2:23–25, which "indicates God's fully entering the narrative as the primary character."[5] The Israelites, groaning in distress, "cried out." The record does not even say that they cried out to God. It does say that their outcry "ascended to" God, that he heard it, that he remembered his covenant with the patriarchs, and that he saw them and knew.

For this last verb, the NKJV has "acknowledged them"; NIV, "was concerned about them"; NASB, "took notice of them." Regardless of which rendering is closest to the meaning of the Hebrew original, the point is fairly obvious.[6] As Terence Fretheim observes, in reference to this crucial passage, "The God who acts in the narrative is understood to be the kind of God portrayed here."[7]

What theology, what truth(s) about God, should the reader take from this? Without attempting to be exhaustive, I think several things are obvious.

First, God was aware of what was going on in time and space. His infinite apartness—his transcendence, his "wholly otherness"—does not rule this out.

Second, God responded to Israel's circumstances and outcry, and he did so in the context of temporal conditions, in a way that provides consciousness of past and present (at least) and of the difference between the two tenses.

Third, God exhibited personal capacities, and any anthropomorphism in the report must not mitigate the significance of this fact.

In short, the reader correctly assigns ultimate meaning to the sequence of events: (1) the people of Israel were in miserable enslavement; (2) as a

---

[5] Owens, "Free, Present, and Faithful," 621.

[6] Carl Friederich Keil and Franz Delitzsch, "The Second Book of Moses (Exodus)," in *Old Testament Commentaries* (Grand Rapids: Associated Publishers and Authors, 2000), 1:334, render "God noticed them" (cf. NASB) adding, "God's notice has all the energy of love and pity."

[7] Terence E. Fretheim, "Suffering God and Sovereign God in Exodus: A Collision of Images," *Horizons in Biblical Theology* 11 (January 1989): 31–56, 38. Fretheim uses "suffering" broadly to represent a number of qualities, including "genuine interaction with the world" (53n3). Although Fretheim views Scripture from a higher-critical perspective, some of his observations are insightful.

result, they cried out in distress; (3) as a result, God responded—and did, indeed, set in motion a chain of events that would lead to Israel's deliverance (although this last is to be seen in the following narrative rather than here). Nothing about God's decisions and knowledge in eternity is referenced or required to understand this highly theological report.

The Call of Moses

The immediate result of God's response takes the form of his issuing a call to the man who will be the human instrument of Israel's redemption. Again, little time is wasted; Moses, already introduced in chapter 2, is that man, and he is tending the flock of his father-in-law near the great Mount Horeb (Exod 3:1). Events move quickly at first, almost staccato-like.

- The angel of the Lord "appeared" (without being seen) in the flame of a bush burning but not being burned up.
- Moses, observing and marveling, is determined to get nearer to investigate.
- Yahweh, when he saw Moses approaching, addressed him by name.
- Moses (no doubt with fear and trembling) responded, "Here I am."
- Yahweh told him to come no nearer and to remove his sandals on the holy ground; then he identified himself as the God of Moses's father and of the patriarchs.
- Moses, understandably, hid his face in fear.

At this point, the narrative slows for the important interchange between God and Moses.

First God speaks, with noteworthy verbs of action. He has "observed" and heard Israel's situation (v. 7; cf. v. 9). As a result he has "come down" to deliver them from Egypt to a bountiful land (v. 8). He is "sending" Moses to them for this purpose (v. 10).

Moses lodges his first objection, to which God responds that he "will" be with him and bring him and the people back to Horeb (vv. 11–12). Moses asks how to identify the Lord, who reveals himself to be I AM, without explaining the implications. Surely this entails, at the least, that he really exists and is eternal and unchanging (vv. 13–14).[8] Moses is to go and gather Israel's elders and tell them that this is the God who has sent him to them, that Yahweh has "appeared" and "paid close attention" to their affliction and will certainly "bring them up" from their misery (vv. 15–17). The verbs have interesting implications.

At this point, notice that the Lord is speaking with certainty about the future. He will deliver them and bring them to Canaan (v. 17). They will heed Moses's voice (v. 18). The king of Egypt will not let them go (v. 19), which introduces a famous question about the hardening of Pharaoh, to which I will return shortly. In response to Pharaoh's resistance, the Lord will act: he will strike Egypt and execute judgment in the form of miraculous plagues—after which the Egyptians, in whose eyes Israel will find favor, will let them go (vv. 20–22). That God has exhaustive foreknowledge is clear; only part of this is what he himself intends to do. It is also clear that he is in control and his purpose will not fail: "God's sovereignty is evident in the divine initiative, the setting of the agenda, the will to deliver Israel, and the announced ability to accomplish this."[9]

Chapter 4 continues the interchange. Moses offers that the people might not believe that Yahweh has sent him, and God responds with signs he can use (vv. 1–9). Moses sees a problem in his inability to speak easily and well, and God promises Aaron to speak for him (vv. 10–17), reminding Moses that God is the one who has made the mouths and ears and eyes of human beings (v. 11).

Moses, setting forth on the mission God gave him, returned to Egypt (vv. 18–31). On the way, God "confronted him and intended to put him

---

[8] Owens, "Free, Present, and Faithful," 622, approvingly cites Martin Buber, who translates this as "I will be present howsoever I will be present," and suggests that it focuses on God as present in his own freedom and who cannot be conjured up by creatures, thus contrasting Yahweh with all the gods who are no gods.

[9] Fretheim, "Suffering God," 38.

to death," perhaps by serious illness (vv. 24–26). It is not necessary to comment in detail about this otherwise unique incident, except to say (in keeping with the purpose of this work) that it strongly supports the notion that God acts in time and space.

What, then, does this passage about the call of Moses impart to our theology? Start with the truths already noted in connection with 2:23–25. God is very much aware and active, as a personal being, in the temporal world we inhabit. The rhetorical questions in 4:11 show, for example, that it is utter foolishness to think that the God who made humans' mouths, ears, and eyes does not himself speak, hear, and see. It is ridiculous, then, to affirm—as some theologians have—that God cannot speak to us in human language and give us truth about himself. It is likewise ridiculous, in view of the fact that God has created this world of time and space, to suggest that he cannot act within its framework, as it functions. Everything in this passage speaks loudly to the contrary.

To be sure, God is I AM, the God who—in contrast to idols—really exists and is eternal and unchanging. He is also the one who sees and hears and responds, who "comes down" to take a hand in human affairs, who meets Moses at a specific geographic location and speaks to him from the space of a bush on fire, and who calls and commissions Moses. He is also a God of foreknowledge who is in control. He not only knows what he himself will do but what Pharaoh will do and what Israel will do. He will succeed in bringing about the deliverance of Israel from Egypt into freedom in a land promised to the patriarchs.

The passage is theologically rich, informing us both about God's eternal nature ("I AM") and foreknowledge, and about his involvement with us in our world, "sensing" our condition, giving us mission, acting in our behalf in one moment or another, fully conscious of past, present, and future. And all of God's "this-worldness" is just as real, with the meaning inherent in the record, as his eternal being. His foreknowledge, for example, does not prevent him from genuine interaction with us in our freedom.

The Contest with Pharaoh, Part I: Who Hardened His Heart?

The matter of Pharaoh's stubborn resistance to God's voice, mediated through Moses and Aaron, makes for a heated argument among interpreters of Scripture. Did God harden Pharaoh's heart, and if so, what does that mean? Did Pharaoh's resistance arise from within himself, unprovoked and uncaused by God? Who started it?

The initial reference appears in 3:19–20, when God said to Moses even before the latter yielded to the mission God chose him for: "I know that the king of Egypt will not allow you to go, even under force from a strong hand. But when I stretch out my hand and strike Egypt with all my miracles that I will perform in it, after that, he will let you go." From the very beginning, then, it was certain that Pharaoh was not going to yield to Yahweh's demands without a serious struggle.

This declaration does not speak to the question why that was so or who was responsible, although one can easily read it to imply that the resistance arose within Pharaoh's own will. Regardless, a theology of divine foreknowledge is plainly in view. God knows both what Pharaoh will do, at two different stages, and what he himself will do. While the record at this point does not rule out the possibility that God directly acted to stiffen Pharaoh's resistance, we more naturally read it to report God's knowledge of Pharaoh's own free decisions.

Following this, a series of statements across the narrative refers to the hardening of Pharaoh's heart.

- 4:21: "I (Yahweh) will harden his heart so that he won't let the people go." Said to Moses even before his return to Egypt, immediately after the Lord reminded him to be sure to do, before Pharaoh, the "wonders" with which he had gifted him.
- 5:2: "Pharaoh responded, 'Who is the LORD that I should obey him by letting Israel go? I don't know the LORD, and besides, I will not let Israel go'." Said in response to Moses's first appearance before

him, requesting release for Israel. While nothing is said about hardening, the words clearly depict willful resistance on Pharaoh's part.

- 7:3: "I will harden Pharaoh's heart and multiply my signs and wonders in the land of Egypt." Said to Moses when the Lord instructed him to go to Pharaoh for a second time, after the latter had increased the burdens of the Israelites in response to the first request.

- 7:13–14: "Pharaoh's heart was hard, and he did not listen to them, as the LORD had said. Then the LORD said to Moses, 'Pharaoh's heart is hard: He refuses to let the people go.'" Said after Moses performed wonders on the occasion of his and Aaron's second appearance before Pharaoh.

- 7:22: "Pharaoh's heart was hard, and he would not listen to them, as the LORD had said." Said after Egypt's waters were turned to blood (first plague).

- 8:15: "When Pharaoh saw there was relief, he hardened his heart and would not listen to them, as the LORD had said." Said when the frogs (second plague) were gone.

- 8:19: "Pharaoh's heart was hard, and he would not listen to them, as the LORD had said." Said when Egypt's magicians could not match the (third) plague of lice and informed Pharaoh that the plague was Yahweh's doing.

- 8:32: "Pharaoh hardened his heart this time also and did not let the people go." Said after the fleas (fourth plague) were removed; this plague (and subsequent ones) did not touch Israel.

- 9:7: "Pharaoh's heart was hard, and he did not let the people go." Said after the pestilence on the Egyptians' livestock (fifth plague).

- 9:12: "The LORD hardened Pharaoh's heart and he did not listen to them, as the LORD had told Moses." Said after the onset of the boils (sixth plague).

- 9:16–17: "I have let you live for this purpose: to show you my power and to make my name known on the whole earth. You are still acting arrogantly against my people by not letting them go." Said to Pharaoh in announcing the (seventh) plague of hail.

- 9:34–35: "When Pharaoh saw that the rain, hail, and thunder had ceased, he sinned again and hardened his heart, he and his officials. So Pharaoh's heart was hard, and he did not let the Israelites go, as the Lord had said through Moses." Said when the hail had ended.
- 10:1: "The Lord said to Moses, 'Go to Pharaoh, for I have hardened his heart and the hearts of his officials so that I may do these miraculous signs of mine among them.'" Said in preparation for the locusts (eighth plague).
- 10:20: "The Lord hardened Pharaoh's heart, and he did not let the Israelites go." Said after the locusts were taken away.
- 10:27: "The Lord hardened Pharaoh's heart, and he was unwilling to let them go." Said after the (ninth) plague of darkness.
- 11:1: "The Lord said to Moses, 'I will bring one more plague on Pharaoh and on Egypt. After that, he will let you go from here.'" Said between the ninth and tenth plagues.
- 11:10: "The Lord hardened Pharaoh's heart, and he would not let the Israelites go out of his land." Said as a summing up of events up to the point just before the tenth plague, the death of the firstborn.
- 14:4: "I will harden Pharaoh's heart so that he will pursue them. Then I will receive glory by means of Pharaoh and all his army, and the Egyptians will know that I am the Lord." Said after Israel left Egypt but before the crossing of the Red Sea.
- 14:8: "The Lord hardened the heart of Pharaoh king of Egypt, and he pursued the Israelites, who were going out defiantly." Said at the same time as the preceding.

What is one to make of this essentially unique biblical record? The following observations are justified.

First, it appears obvious that both Pharaoh and God were active in hardening Pharaoh's heart. "God's activity hardens Pharaoh's own obduracy to the point of no return."[10] In nine of the eighteen mentions

---

[10] Fretheim, "Suffering God," 43.

of this hardening, God is the doer, and in nine either Pharaoh hardened his heart (three times) or (impersonally) his heart was, grew, or became hard (six times).

Second, the direct responsibility of Pharaoh himself is indicated in various ways. In 3:19, before the encounter begins, "*the king of Egypt* will not allow you to go" (emphasis added). In 5:2 Pharaoh declares his indifference to Yahweh. In 7:13–14, the statements that he did not heed Moses and Aaron and refused their request appear to exegete the statement that his heart was hardened—as in several other verses. In 9:17 the Lord said that Pharaoh was "acting arrogantly."

Third, an objective reading of the account leaves one unable to avoid concluding that God deliberately acted with the intention of hardening Pharaoh's heart. The question, then, is what this means. It could mean, perhaps, that the Lord directly influenced Pharaoh's will—like flipping a switch within him, similar to brain surgery—to reject the request. One who thinks this is what happened may quote Prov 21:1: "A king's heart is like channeled water in the LORD's hand: / He directs it wherever he chooses."

But this is by no means a necessary reading of the account, nor would it accord with the agency of Pharaoh. Instead, the more likely meaning is that the Lord intentionally acted in such a way that he knew Pharaoh would respond to in increasingly stubborn resistance. If this is the correct reading, Prov 21:1 will apply equally as well.

This does not absolve God of responsibility, of course, and neither does it absolve Pharaoh. Nor does it interfere with Pharaoh's freedom. Instead—and this is most important—it shows that God was judging Pharaoh (and Egypt), as the entire account makes clear. Before anything transpired, God knew that Pharaoh's will was such that he would not heed the request or the warnings or the plagues—not until the death of the firstborn. Such a judgment situation, involving the specific matter of releasing Israel, does not directly apply to God's regular way of dealing with human beings, especially in regard to their salvation. But God does act, in some circumstances, to influence men toward hardening in judgment; see 2 Thess 2:9–12 for a clear example of this principle.

The Contest with Pharaoh, Part II:
The Acts of God in Time and Space

The account of the struggle to obtain Israel's release from Egypt is replete with explicit references to the acts of God in the temporal world of Moses and Pharaoh, the Egyptians and the Israelites. The narrative is, above everything else, a recounting of what God did on earth in time. Since there is too much of this for comment on everything, I will speak primarily of categories, which are telling.

First, over and over we read that the Lord spoke, said, or replied to Moses. Considering Exodus 5–12 as the primary record of the contest and Israel's departure, this otherwise innocuous little statement occurs some twenty times, starting in 6:1. It puts the account on the correct footing as what Yahweh was orchestrating at the time in Egypt, and it clearly witnesses to God's active ability to communicate with Moses in the latter's time and space.

Second, numerous first-person speeches of the Lord are recorded in the account, and in them he shows mastery of the temporal context and of how to use the past, present, and future tenses in his own words.[11] In 6:3–8, for example, the Lord speaks of what he had done in the past—"I appeared" (to the patriarchs) and "established my covenant" (with them); of what he has only now done—"I have heard the groaning" of the children of Israel and "remembered my covenant"; and of what he will do in the future—"I will bring you out . . . will take you as my people . . . [and] will bring you to the land."

Among other examples of this is 7:1–5, which also demonstrates the Lord's awareness of the relationship between one temporal event and another: "The Egyptians will know that I am the LORD *when* I stretch out my hand against Egypt and bring out the Israelites from among them"

---

[11] Although the Hebrew tenses are not fundamentally temporal, the translations (including the Greek Septuagint and English versions) have generally rendered the meaning correctly.

(emphasis added). God's eternity does not prevent him from being aware of and involved in events in time and space.

Third, the account frequently declares that the plagues were the Lord's doing, often by his own affirmation. For example, in 9:5 the Lord himself says, "Tomorrow the LORD will do this thing in the land" (bring pestilence on the cattle of the Egyptians)—showing both his understanding of the details of time and space and his direct agency. Compare 9:18: "Tomorrow at this time I will rain down the worst hail that has ever occurred in Egypt from the day it was founded until now"; see also 9:14, 23. Clearly, the plagues were acts of the Lord, and the record intends for us to recognize them as such.

Fourth, throughout the account we are meant to understand many things the Lord does in response to what has been done by others. Thus we are reading about interaction, not unilateral actions. From the start, as already noted, the Lord said, "I know that the king of Egypt will not let you go unless a mighty hand compels him. So I will stretch out my hand and strike the Egyptians with all the wonders that I will perform among them. After that, he will let you go" (3:19–20 NIV).[12] In 6:5, the Lord represents his coming deliverance as a response to the fact that he had "heard the groaning of the Israelites." In 8:2 the Lord instructs Moses to tell Pharaoh, "If you refuse to let them go, then I will plague all your territory with frogs" (cf. 8:21).

Furthermore, there are times when the Lord acts in response to what Moses says to him, as in 8:12–13: "Moses cried out to the LORD for help concerning the frogs. . . . The LORD did as Moses had said" (cf. 8:31; 7:1; etc.). The entire narrative is couched as influence and response; we should take this mode of interaction at full face value.

Comments about the theological implications of this part of the narrative will appear at the conclusion of this chapter.

---

[12] "So" is the Hebrew *waw*, but even if translated "And" the meaning would be the same, that the Lord's judgments will fall in consequence of Pharaoh's refusal.

From Egypt to Sinai

It is not necessary to comment on every detail of the journey from Egypt to Sinai and beyond. Little more than a brief listing of the major elements of the narrative is needed to highlight the pattern.

- Exodus 13 makes provision for future memorializing of the deliverance in the annual Passover celebration. The Israelites will tell their children that the Lord "with a strong hand" brought them out of Egypt (vv. 8–9) and that "the LORD killed every firstborn male" of the Egyptians (v. 15).

- Exodus 13:21 describes a special provision that Yahweh made when Israel began the journey out of Egypt: "The LORD went before them by day in a pillar of cloud to lead the way, and by night in a pillar of fire to give them light" (NKJV). Indeed, this continued on to Sinai and beyond.

- The description of God's actions at the Red Sea is dramatic and direct: "The LORD looked down . . . threw the Egyptian forces into confusion . . . caused their chariot wheels to swerve . . . [and] saved Israel." And Israel "saw the great power that the LORD used against the Egyptians" (14:24–31). The song in chapter 15 sounds this note repeatedly.

- The provision of manna was the action of God: "I am going to rain bread from heaven for you" (16:4). "It is the bread the LORD has given you to eat" (v. 15).

- Especially dramatic is the scene at Sinai in Exodus 19–20. God "answered him [Moses] in the thunder" ("by voice," NKJV) and "came down on Mount Sinai at the top of the mountain" (19:19–20). Then he spoke in the hearing of all the Israelites the Ten Commandments (20:1; cf. v. 19). Furthermore, these commandments were given in written form on two stone tablets, which "were the work of God, and the writing was God's writing, engraved on the tablets" (32:16).

- When the covenant had been ratified, Moses and the first priests—Aaron and his two sons—and seventy elders of the new nation ascended the mountain, "and they saw the God of Israel. Beneath his feet was something like a pavement made of lapis lazuli, as clear as the sky itself" (24:9–10).

- Following this, "the glory of the LORD settled on Mount Sinai," and "the appearance of the LORD's glory to the Israelites was like a consuming fire" (vv. 16–17).

- Exodus 32 describes the tragic events involved in Israel's breaking of the covenant in the matter of the golden calf.[13] God's wrath burned hot (v. 11), and he said he would consume Israel and start over with Moses (v. 10), but Moses interceded (vv. 11–13) and "the LORD relented concerning the disaster he said he would bring on his people" (v. 14). "In the act of changing his mind, God's immutability is established."[14] Moses's pleading on behalf of the people continued (v. 31), and finally the Lord spoke to Moses "face to face" (33:11) and in the end promised, "My presence will go with you" (v. 14).[15]

- In consequence of Moses's pleading for confirmation of this promise, the Lord manifested himself to Moses in a unique way, saying, "Here is a place near me. You are to stand on the rock, and when my glory passes by, I will put you in the crevice of the rock and cover you with my hand until I have passed by. Then I will take my hand away, and you will see my back, but my face will not be seen" (33:21–23).

- Then the Lord instructed Moses to prepare two tablets of stone and bring them to him, promising to "write on them the words

---

[13] Owens, "Free, Present, and Faithful," 625, insightfully observes, "They worshipped him as if he were one of the conjurable gods, a god whose power can be harnessed by the appropriate images and incantations."

[14] Owens, 626.

[15] Fretheim, "Suffering God," 41, notes enticingly that God had entered into such a relationship with Moses that God was not the only one who had something to say; so did Moses.

that were on the first tablets." Moses obeyed, and the Lord "came down in a cloud, stood with him there, and proclaimed his name, 'the LORD.' The LORD passed in front of him and proclaimed . . ." (34:1, 5–6). Not to be missed is the way the Lord describes himself here (vv. 6–7), which is the very model of a God who relates himself to the world and to those who bear his image and whom he has placed here.

The covenant was thus restored.

Anyone familiar with the account will recognize that I have only mentioned highlights and have done so with deliberate brevity. No doubt it would be easy to multiply this material at considerable length.

Implications for Speaking about God (Theology)

The deliverance of Israel from Egyptian bondage is the redemption story of the Old Testament. As Tomes observes:

> In the Old Testament it is the exodus from Egypt which is thought to reveal God's nature and purpose most significantly. This was the event above all others which established Israel's relationship with Yahweh, as His chosen people, delivered entirely by His mercy and power, and bound to Him thereafter by ties of gratitude and filial fear. . . . Most significantly of all, the memory of it was kept fresh each year by its commemoration at Passover.[16]

Christians look back on the death, burial, resurrection, and ascension of Jesus Christ as the crisis redemption event of their salvation history. Just so, the people of God of the former covenant reveled in the acts of God in freeing them from Egypt as the redemption event that sealed their covenant relationship with Yahweh as his people.

---

[16] Tomes, "Exodus 14," 456.

So what theology do we learn from this survey of the Exodus story? Much in every way; here is some of that theology that bears on the theme of this book.

First, there is no avoiding the clear impression that God was the chief actor, that he was orchestrating events in accord with his own purpose, that he himself was at work, acting from outside but within the realm of time and space. At the same time, the record indicates full respect for and recognition of the agency of the human beings with whom God was interacting, including Moses and Pharaoh.

Second, necessary to this is the fact that God was acting in our world. The record, as reviewed, leaves no doubt about God's ability to do this. Some of the language is almost visceral, and while it incorporates many anthropomorphic elements, the nature of the descriptions is such that it cannot be entirely anthropomorphic. God may not have a mouth, but he spoke at specific times and in identified places, in the ordinary hearing of human beings. He has no body parts, no face or back or feet, but people saw with their eyes what they understood to be representations of God's presence. It must be the case, then, at the least, that God, acting in this world, caused physical phenomena to appear in space and time. The God we see acting in Exodus is the eternal God acting; no other representation of him is needed.

Third, God was fully comfortable, and accurate, in using the terminology of time, for example. He knew the difference between today and tomorrow, understood the past and the future, and used tensed statements to anchor his own acts in time, also linking them to spatial locations. None of this is surprising, of course, for the Creator of this space-time realm.

Fourth, equally clear is the fact that the account is referring to events that transpired in this world at the specific times and places indicated. The record makes no statement and implies nothing about what might have eternally existed in the will and purpose of God. There, in Egypt and at Sinai and on the way, all these things occurred. Then and there God and Moses and Pharaoh and Israel were active, each in responsible ways. The events are represented as themselves having the significance attributed to them, not as playing out unseen designs foreordained by God forever.

Fifth, to be sure, we cannot help feeling that the God who was operating in Egypt and at the Red Sea and in the wilderness from there to Sinai is a God who was fulfilling a settled purpose that is as eternal as he is. But when we have gathered this implication, we are obligated, I believe, to read that eternal purpose through the lens of what is revealed as having actually transpired in time and space, not vice versa.[17] This is where God reveals himself in action and in the relation between his actions and the actions of others. Consequently, this is where he reveals his one and only purpose for Israel and Moses and Egypt and Pharaoh. We should therefore understand that God's eternal purpose was to do exactly what he did and in the way he did: to interact with Pharaoh and the Egyptians, and with Moses and Israel, in the very way the action is described in the inspired record—in an influence-and-response mode, in other words.

I repeat: the God at work in Exodus is God at work in eternity, and these two are one and the same. We should define his eternal acts and knowledge to match what we see here.

Owens makes some helpful comments along these lines.

> The languages of philosophical theology and the biblical narrative are extraordinarily different. While theology seeks to discipline its language in order to speak as precisely as possible the biblical narrative paints in broad, anthropomorphic brush strokes. . . . Both want to distinguish God from God's creation, show God as radically present and utterly free, and affirm that God does not change. Exodus does this through the narrative heightening and resolving of tension regarding God's character and identity; classical Christian theology by employing the language of metaphysics to distinguish God from that which God has created. It is a mistake to pit one against the

---

[17] Fretheim, "Suffering God," 45, perceptively notes that one problem for some theologians is that they read the metaphors of sovereignty as being (exclusively) univocal, and that this easily leads to a form of idolatry. I suspect he is saying something similar to what I am saying but in an entirely different way.

other. Rather, they are both doing largely the same thing in a way appropriate to each.[18]

I agree with Owens, but I would add that we can read the theology of the biblical record more clearly than the theology of what Owens calls "apophatic" metaphysical reasoning.[19] If a theologian thinks first of God as he or she has conceived him to be in his eternal existence, and then reads the biblical record in the light of that conception, the theologian may very well misunderstand both the record and God. A theologian who is a determinist, for example, will read the account to mean that each event is a necessity, predetermined by God, including the choices and actions of human beings. In contrast, a theologian who begins with the inspired account of what happened will more likely see the events as contingencies involving humans making self-determined choices. Then God in eternity can be understood as sovereignly designing humans to exercise libertarian freedom, at the same time effectively achieving his own eternal purposes.

---

[18] Owens, "Free, Present, and Faithful," 626–27.

[19] "Apophatic" means knowledge gained by negation, in this case by rationally affirming what God is not.

THIRTEEN

Creation Theology

I have touched on a wide variety of matters, and the relationship between them should be clear enough. It is time, now, to draw things together and focus on the principal concerns.

In Summary: The Main Points

First, God's creation of the world of time and space, which includes making us in his image and placing us in this world, is an entirely unexpected and stunning thing to consider. Probably no theologian could have logically drawn, from any a priori reasoning about God as he is in eternity, the conclusion that he would do such a thing. God is immutable, and some of the implications of that seem to rule out God's being in a relationship with a realm in which time and space are essential to its structure. Those two things—an eternal and unchanging God and an ever-changing universe and human beings—seem radically different and incompatible.[1]

---

[1] Kevin Hester observes that this is all the more amazing in the implication that the fully self-sufficient God, who does not need us, desires us for a relationship with him—and "at great cost to Godself"!

199

Second, the very first implication of this creation, in light of its incredible reality, is that we must therefore take this world very seriously. This created world is so unlikely that it must be of great significance. Strengthening this judgment is the fact that the revealed Word of God begins and ends here, and in between it is organized around the events that transpire within the framework of time and space. This is where theology begins. The world of men and things, which provides the subject matter of the Bible, is important and real. It is the realm of God's activity, the realm that—for reasons best known to him alone—he chose to make the arena for his works.

Third, a coimplication of this is equally fundamental: our reasoning about the nature of God in himself, in eternity, must be conducted in heavy reliance on how he has revealed himself in his interactions with us and the world, as recorded and interpreted in Holy Scripture. This observation means that we should allow his acts in history to be primary in our thinking, ultimately influencing our a priori, metaphysical reasoning about the kind of being an eternal God must be. After all, it is the God who interacts with us in time and space who has clearly revealed himself in the Bible, while the God of theo-logical reasoning—as helpful as such reasoning can be—is in many respects a human, logical construct.[2]

That fact does not automatically make our construct wrong in every way, of course, but it does mean—as any biblically dependent theologian should agree—that the biblical record must be primary and our logic its servant. In other words, the way the Bible presents God controls our thinking about his eternal nature, not the other way around. And this caution ought to pervade all our God-speech, whether we are discussing his attributes or his eternal decrees or his (fore)knowledge. All these matters must be viewed in light of his interactions with us and the world as interpreted in the Bible.

Fourth, when we speak of God's attributes, then, we do not allow metaphysical reasoning to take away from the biblical language and teaching.

---

[2] Perhaps some readers will think I am relegating reason to a role that is subordinate to revelation—and perhaps in a way I am. I would not quibble about the relative balance between them, nor would I deny that reason has an important role.

In other words, it may well be more important for theologians to speak of God's eyes, as the Bible does, than to assure the church that he has no eyes. Yes, God is incorporeal, and recognizing anthropomorphisms for what they are is important; the church is better off for understanding such constructs. But the Bible's emphasis is on the fact that God sees everything and on the implications of that fact—on the truth that God's eyes are always on us, in other words. It is existentially justifiable that some in the church have long sung, "All along on the road to the soul's true abode, there's an eye watching you." Never mind the shallow lyrics and the "country" twang; the concept is biblically sound.

Fifth, likewise, when we speak of God's knowledge in eternity, whether called foreknowledge or something else, the way the Bible describes the knowledge of God at work in our world ought to provide the basis for understanding his knowledge forever. There is simply no need to make such a bifurcation between God's eternal knowledge of events in time and space and the events themselves that one sees the first as determining the second. Ultimately, the two are one and the same, and we apprehend its meaning in the second.

Certainly, it is important to talk about foreknowledge. It communicates truth to us, especially the truth that God is omniscient and incorporates everything that will transpire into his all-inclusive plan.[3] He has control and we can trust him. As another popular-level song expresses this truth, "I know not what the future holds, but I know who holds the future!" Still, we must likewise take seriously the knowledge that is grounded in, not determinative of, the facts of time and space themselves. Genesis is speaking truth when it represents God as saying to Abraham, "Now I know that you fear me." Did God know this forever? Certainly, but he knew

---

[3] A few instances exist in Scripture when foreknowledge may involve more than mere prescience, in the same way we sometimes use "know" to embrace a relationship and not mere cognition. Thus Rom 8:29 may well mean, "whom he lovingly acknowledged as his own (in eternal election)." But my purpose has been to deal with foreknowledge in its more basic and consistent meaning as knowing in advance.

it in eternity by virtue of the fact that Abraham obeyed him in the real, temporal world. What God knows eternally, and exhaustively, about the course of events in this world he knows from the course of events in this world—not vice versa.

Sixth, the same observations apply when we speak about God's decrees—his eternal decisions about the existence and course of history. I will say more later about the nature of these decisions and how they apply to the world. For now, however, the point is that there is likewise no need to regard God's decisions in eternity as different "events" from his decisive actions in the world of time and space. Neither needs to be denied or diminished in order to establish the other.

I suggested in an earlier chapter that there must be some sort of coincidence or intersection between eternity and time—else there could be no creation by a God in eternity of a world that is not eternal. Consider any speculative framework for defining the nature of that point of identity as what it is: speculation. Even so, the shared identity between eternity and time should be affirmed.

Regardless, when we read any biblical account that represents God as deciding to act in response to human acts, we ought to understand any decision we attribute to eternity in the very same light as shines on it in the Bible. If the narrative represents God as pleased with the repentance of Nineveh, for example, and as deciding to forgo the destruction he had declared, then we should do two things. First, we should take this account at full face value: the Ninevites really did repent and God really did decide, in response, to withhold destruction of the city. Second, we should regard this meaning as the very meaning of any decision God made in eternity. The events in Jonah's day are the real events, the ones in which God has revealed himself. There is no biblical revelation as to the nature of God's eternal decisions about the destruction or sparing of Nineveh. And there is no reason to think that the decision in eternity predetermined or settled what would happen in time. By the events recounted and interpreted in Scripture we learn what God planned in eternity.

Another Biblical Illustration

Along these lines, here is yet one more example of how the Bible should be read and understood. This example, no better or worse than those developed in chapters 5, 6, and 12, involves the biblical record of the great flood, as found in Genesis 6–9. Most important about this account is that it represents God as actively involved in human and earthly affairs, with specific persons and in specific times and places. Here are some instances of this in the record.

- In 6:3 the Lord uttered a judgment in response to the world's situation and spoke in terms of 120 years until that judgment would fall.
- In 6:5 the Lord "saw" or perceived—"took note," we may say—of the nature of the wickedness on earth.
- In 6:6 the Lord was sorry (regretted) and grieved, as a result of this wickedness, that he had made human beings.
- In 6:7, in consequence of his observations, the Lord pronounced specific judgment.
- In 6:8 Noah "found favor" as a result of what the Lord saw in him—his faith.
- In 6:12 the Lord "saw" how corrupt the earth had become.
- In 6:13 the Lord informed Noah that he had decided to "put an end" (another temporal word) to things and instructed him carefully, in the verses following, as to the spatial measurements to use in constructing an ark. God understands and operates in terms of time and space.
- In 6:17 the Lord told Noah that he himself would bring on the flood.
- In 7:1 the Lord spoke to Noah when the time came to enter the ark.
- In 7:3–4 the Lord indicated that he would cause the rain to start in seven days.
- In 7:16 the Lord shut Noah in.

- In 7:23 the Lord destroyed all living things outside the ark (not life-forms whose context for existence is the water).
- In 8:1 God remembered Noah and caused wind to blow to dry the land.
- In 8:15 God spoke to Noah about departing from the ark.
- In 8:21–22 the Lord smelled the "pleasing aroma" of Noah's offering and said to himself that he would never destroy life that way again, promising (in spatial-temporal terms) to maintain the earth's seasons and days and nights.
- In 9:1 God instructed Noah and his sons about life going forward.
- In 9:8–12 God spoke to Noah and his sons about the terms of the new covenant he was making with them, their descendants, and other life-forms on earth. These terms included (1) the sign of the rainbow whenever he would bring clouds, and (2) a time-anchored promise never again to cut off all flesh by means of a flood.

These are adequate as a basis for some important inferences. (1) God was personally interacting with human beings and with the space-time world. He pronounced judgment, caused the rain to come, shut the ark's door, destroyed the rest of mankind in judgment, and even spoke within himself. (2) God understood and acted within the temporal structure involved. He announced "120 years" and scheduled the rain to begin "in seven days," for examples. He understood and made decisions regarding the rest of the earth's history, including a promise about what he would never do again; even "never" is a temporal word.

It is important to read this without putting the actions back into eternity. God did these things then and there, responding to the human situation in the specific time and place of human circumstances. To be sure, the Lord might very well have known about this and made decisions in eternity, but what is important for understanding the narrative is that he was doing this in our world, in the days of Noah who was 600 years old when the rain began. What God knew and decided in eternity was exactly what occurred on that occasion and meant exactly what the biblical record presents it as meaning in the context of human history on earth.

In other words, we should read the account for exactly what it says. Any anthropomorphism in the narrative—and there is plenty—changes nothing about the meaning. In this account, and others like it, reports of what God decided and said and did are expressed in exactly the same way as reports of what human beings decided and said and did in the created world. Both are equally straightforward.

To repeat, the meaning of this series of events is to be determined from what is described in the record as occurring in time and space, not from some a priori definition of God's decrees and knowledge in eternity. Indeed, the opposite is true: what God knew and decided in eternity takes its meaning and can only be understood from this historical event in the biblical record.

In other words, the record means that humanity became so wicked that God decided he must, in judgment, destroy the race and start over. He determined that Noah and his family were candidates for that new beginning and graciously provided for their deliverance and for the preservation of the animal life that would also be destroyed. Then he sent a flood that took the lives of all human beings except for Noah and his family. All of this is influence and response in time and space: God responding to human actions and humans responding to God.[4]

To be sure, deterministic theologians are going to say no to this approach, insisting that the meaning of what happens in time and space is predetermined by what God decided and knew in eternity. But while I do not deny that God foreknew all this and planned for it in eternity, I am convinced that it is the biblical account of what actually transpired that explains

---

[4] My references to "influence and response" reflect the work of Forlines, *Quest for Truth*, 144 (see chap. 1, n. 7); see also "influence and response" in the index of that book. This model represents interaction between God and human beings (and between human beings) as interpersonal in the fullest sense, with each influencing and responding to the other, rather than as a cause-and-effect relationship.

and exposes the nature of God's knowledge and decisions in eternity.[5] The events in time and space are described in clear terms, but God's eternal knowledge and decisions involving this event are not revealed anywhere. So we are left to understand eternity by what actually transpired.

Indeed, I have suggested in an earlier chapter that these two perspectives are not different, in number, after all. The decisions and knowledge in eternity are in some way the same as they are in time and space. We do not need to dichotomize between eternity and the historical event. We need to understand both—if we must think of them as two—by the light in which the biblical record reveals the event in time and space. This is the realm in which God has deigned to act and bring about the achievement of his purposes.

The Nature of the Created World

The key issue, then, is what sort of world God chose to make, what sort of world we live in, what sort of beings we are in the image of God. The issue is not the sovereignty of God. There is no disputing that God is absolutely sovereign and governs the world in full cognizance of, and control of, all that transpires. Whatever sort of world he made, whatever kind of beings we are, he independently and freely determined for all things to be and function as they are and do. For God's sovereignty to be intact requires nothing more than that the universe function in whatever way he has purposed that it function.

Nor is the issue the depravity of mankind since the fall. There is no doubt that man in his depravity is effectively disabled, entirely incapable in his natural condition of turning to God.

The issue is also not whether salvation is by grace through faith. The triune God does all the saving, and man contributes nothing. And all that God does in salvation is in grace, entirely without consideration of any human

---

[5] Kevin Hester suggests that this may accord well with the Reformation insistence on the sufficiency of Scripture.

merit.[6] Salvation is not synergistic; human beings do not "work" together with God to provide or apply salvation.[7]

No, the issue is what sort of world God created this world to be and how it relates to him in eternity. To express this issue in traditional terms, it is whether God designed his world in such a way that determinism or (libertarian) freedom prevails in the moral actions of human beings. This is not an issue of divine sovereignty since whichever way the world operates, it does so by the free pleasure of God, who made it to operate the way it does. The only question is whether God designed us to exercise freedom or to will only what he has first made necessary for us to will.

This means, then, that the issue is whether we take the biblical record to mean what it seems clearly to mean: that God created human beings with the responsibility to make moral choices, that he sets before them options and then allows them to choose, and that he condemns or justifies them in response to the choices they make.[8]

This is, then, the long-term debate between determinism and free will. And when I say "free will" I mean what the philosophers and theologians call libertarian freedom. Since I do not believe that anything less than libertarian freedom—or the power of alternative choice—is truly freedom, I may well use the word *freedom* with this meaning.[9]

---

[6] I have dealt with these issues fully elsewhere and do not wish to treat them again here. See Picirilli, *Free Will Revisited* (see chap. 5, n. 4).

[7] See chapter 15, "Are Arminians Semi-Pelagians and Synergists Who Deny Total Depravity and Natural Inability?" in Matthew Pinson, *40 Questions about Arminianism* (Grand Rapids: Kregel, forthcoming), for a helpful discussion of synergism versus monergism and all aspects of a sound Arminian soteriology.

[8] This is a dreadful oversimplification. I am sure that fallen human beings, when faced with the choice between submitting to God and resisting his advances, must resist unless God in his grace enables a positive response by the work of his Word and Holy Spirit. Yet this is a work that opens and does not close the door to *either* choice. See Picirilli, *Grace, Faith, Free Will* (see preface, n. 4); also my *Free Will Revisited*.

[9] I do not do this arrogantly. I understand that compatibilists believe they give "freedom" an adequate meaning when they define it as voluntarily (not by

It seems clear that those who reject such a view of freedom do so, at least in part, because they believe they are exalting God in attributing to him the ultimate responsibility for everything that occurs in the universe. Among other things involved in this is the question of whether God has an eternal, all-inclusive plan for the history of the world and humankind, one that must in fact be achieved. The opposite of that possibility is, of course, that his plan or purpose for us (and the world) must be thwarted. I am satisfied that God has an eternal, all-inclusive plan for the world and for humankind, and that he inevitably achieves his purposes.

So, the question becomes this: Can God have and achieve an all-inclusive plan if humans have real moral freedom? In order to achieve success, did God have to make decisions in eternity about the moral choices to be made by human beings in history? Did God's decisions in eternity determine what human choices must be—that is, that the choices are necessary, the only choices each person is able to make? This view is called "determinism," and it means that the events in the real world were all settled by the decisions (decrees) of God in eternity. This way, all events in the real world are secondary to God's eternal decisions and take their meaning from those decisions. This is not the view expressed in this work.

Instead, I am affirming that God can incorporate everything that occurs in history, including all the free acts of human beings, into his plan and still be certain to achieve success without binding human beings under necessity. Let us suppose, then, that it was and is the will of God that human beings have freedom of choice and that he created the race and the world to function in accord with that will. Let us suppose, also, that he foreknew the fall and determined to send his Son to make an atonement intended to provide for the salvation of the entire human race, and then to offer to all of them the option of receiving or rejecting that Savior and the salvation he purchased. Let us suppose, further, that he recognized their helplessness even to accept such an offer without his grace and provided his Word and the convicting work of

---

compulsion) doing the one thing that the person really can do because he or she strongly wants to do that.

the Holy Spirit with it to open their blind eyes and enable them, otherwise disabled, to make a true choice between the alternatives, without overpowering their ability to reject him even then. Finally, let us suppose that he applies the redemption offered to those who receive his Son in genuine, saving faith.

The question is, then, Can God maintain control in such a world? Can he guarantee the success of his all-inclusive plan if he creates human beings to make the choice between accepting and rejecting his provision? The answer is yes. Without discounting the reality of God's knowledge and decisions in eternity, we can view God as so all-capable that he can effect the success of his plan without foreordaining or predetermining human choices in such a way as to make them necessary, the only choices possible.

For a starting point, consider how a capable human being works. Settling on a plan (for a business, say, or for some other project), he proceeds to put it into effect, knowing that many true contingencies will arise, including the free choices of others who must be put into play. At every step along the way, things over which he has no control develop one way or another. Other people who are involved make choices, good and bad, some helpful and some detrimental to the advancement of the plan. He responds as the occasions arise. He is experienced and can read people well. Some of the setbacks that develop he has envisioned and made plans to deal with. Others he has to find solutions for after they occur unexpectedly. Sometimes he improvises, unsure of the outcome. But he is capable, and throughout the process, with its disappointments and successes, he makes steady progress and ultimately achieves his plan. In this kind of eventuality, the actual actions of this person and others involved are really happening. The success is real in spite of the contingencies. We may even say that the plan was the concept, not the reality.

I am not saying that this is the way God works. I am saying, however, that even if God were working in that way, he is all-capable and could be expected to succeed regardless of the ups and downs along the way. In God's case, however, the prospects are far better than this. He not only "could be expected to" but certainly will succeed. He has unlimited resources at his disposal to guarantee this.

- He has foreknowledge, knowing exactly what every person will choose and incorporating that into his plan.
- He has what Molina (unnecessarily) called middle knowledge, knowing just how every human being will respond in every conceivable circumstance, and he is in control of the circumstances.
- He knows counterfactuals and can use that knowledge to his advantage—essentially the same as the preceding point.
- He is omnipotent and is able to control all the forces of nature, for example.
- His providence is all-inclusive, so that he governs the world in accord with his plan—his will, in other words. He arranges the circumstances of the lives of those who are his for their benefit as well as the circumstances of all his creatures—humans included— for his purposes. His purposes include sustaining all creatures to be what he created them to be. As the twentieth-century folk song reminds us, "He's got the whole world in his hands."
- He fully knows and respects human beings as he has constituted them in his image and therefore lovingly applies everything at his disposal to maintain them as he created them—as free moral agents who make real choices that he does not constrain by manipulating them or making their choices necessary ones.
- The world he has made, then, is a world where God and human beings are "persons." As such, they interact in an influence-and-response mode, not in a cause-and-effect mode.[10] God acts and people respond freely to submit or resist. People act and God responds accordingly. The relationship is loving, communicating, interpersonal.

---

[10] I have commented earlier on the fact that philosophically minded theologians use the word *cause* in different senses. What I am saying here lies outside that discussion. Certainly, God upholds our very existence at all times, so that life and breath and choices would be otherwise impossible. But he does not cause our choices in a way that makes them necessary, that limits us to the ones we make (compatibilism).

It may well be that this view exalts God's greatness and power even more than determinism. Even if God should have to make adjustments in the details as he goes along, depending on human responses, we can be certain that he will fully accomplish his purposes. But it is clear that he, foreknowing everything, does not have to do that.

There is no question, then, that God's all-inclusive purpose will be successful. When he determined to create the world, he knew all the possibilities and actualized the world that is, one that achieves his purposes. Even persons who reject him and are consigned to eternal punishment fulfill his will in one sense: they choose their own destiny. All moral wrongs—all sins, in other words—are committed in accord with his will that human beings have moral freedom and responsibility. When he created the world, he saw all this in its future and actualized it. In doing so, he did not make any of these choices, or the choices of those who submit to him, necessary. But he knew what they would choose and willed for them that freedom.

In such a world as this, it is the events of human history in time and space that are real. The plan in eternity is important, to be sure, but the outworking of that plan in time and space is the actual achievement.

This is the way we ought to speak about God.

A Final Word about Theology

Informally, now, I am speaking directly to my readers—as I have said, we are all theologians—with a concluding word that can more or less sum up my primary purpose. I was just reading, in my daily devotional time, Genesis 25, which describes the birth of the twins Jacob and Esau. As I was reading slowly, out loud, mulling over the text from verse to verse, I came to v. 21: "Isaac prayed to the LORD on behalf of his wife because she was childless. The LORD was receptive to his prayer, and his wife Rebekah conceived."

There it was again. Then and there, in whatever year BC and whatever day Isaac marked on the calendar that hung on his wall, two things transpired. (1) Isaac pleaded with God about Rebekah's barrenness. (Probably not for the first time!) (2) God heard and, as a result, acted—in time and

space—to enable Rebekah to conceive. Both clauses have exactly the same
ultimate, metaphysical meaning. Isaac prayed. God answered. The two
propositions communicate the same way and should be read alike. The text
is not referring to anything God did "in eternity." Whatever he does in time
is what he does in eternity.

Let no theology lessen the impact and meaning of the biblical narrative.
Isaac prayed to God from time and space. And God listened and determined to act in time and space. No other meaning is needed. Any other
meaning is eisegesis.

I urge every theologian: do not push this back into eternity, which is
not the locus of the event. The best theology book of all, the Bible, does not
even mention implications for eternity. If we push it back there somewhere,
we will invest it with a meaning different from the meaning God reveals in
describing it. We would presume to do that.

Sure, we will do our school theology. There is something important
about that. But what is even more important is to let the Bible teach theology, and here it teaches—as straightforwardly as possible—that Isaac asked
God and God granted his request. That is the beautiful theology we uncover
here. If our school theology leads us to read into this something from an
a priori understanding of God, including his decrees and knowledge, which
adjusts the meaning of this ever so slightly, we have misrepresented God.
God has revealed what he wants us to know about Isaac and Rebekah,
and about prayer and its answer, and about time and space, and about the
immutable God who creates a world as a stage for his actions.

This truly biblical theology, then, ought to affect how we understand,
speak, and reason about the God of eternity, not the other way around. Let
the fact that Isaac prayed and God acted in response, which is the theology
revealed in the passage, be the understanding in the light of which everything else is measured. And let us worship him and emulate Isaac.

Author Index

213

SCRIPTURE INDEX

215

Psalms

10:11 *7*
11:4 *6–7*
33 *46*
33:6 *46*
33:9 *46*
78 *51*
78:1–8 *51*
78:9–11 *51*
78:12–13 *51*
78:14 *51*
78:15–16 *52*
78:17–25 *52*
78:26–31 *52*
78:32–33 *52*
78:34–39 *52*
78:40–53 *52*
78:54–58 *52*
78:59–64 *52*
78:65–72 *52*
90:2 *38*
94:8–9 *7*
94:8–10 *28*
95 *54*
95:8–9 *55*
95:10 *55*
95:11 *55*
99 *55*
99:6 *55*
99:7 *55*
102:2 *56*
105 *53*
106 *53*
106:7 *53*
106:8 *53*
106:12 *53*
106:13–14 *53*
106:15 *53*
106:23 *53*
106:44–45 *53*
131:1 *106*

Proverbs

21:1 *190*

Isaiah

38 *69*
38:1 *70*
59:1 *6*

Jeremiah

18 *71, 74*
18:1–3 *71*
18:1–12 *71*
18:4 *71*
18:5–10 *71*
18:6 *72*
18:7–8 *72*
18:7–10 *74*
18:9–10 *72*
18:11 *72*
18:11–12 *72*
18:12 *72–73*
18:15 *72*
21:8 *50*
36 *87*
36:3 *88*
36:7 *88*
38:17–23 *146*
38:18 *146*

Ezekiel

33:11 *171*

Hosea

11:8–9 *10–11*

Jonah

3 *66*
3:4 *67*
3:5–9 *67*
3:10 *14, 67*

Zechariah

8:14 *15*

Malachi

3:6 *14*